No Wishing Required:

The Business Case for
Project Assurance

Randy,

I hope you enjoy The book.

Best wishes for continued success!

ISBN: 0983033544
ISBN-13: 9780983033547

No Wishing Required:

The Business Case for Project Assurance

Rob Prinzo

THE STORY BEHIND
No Wishing Required

E VER WISH THAT you had done something differently? Sure, we all have. But you can't change the past; you can only change the present and the future, which is why I wrote this book. It's about collaborative intervention[SM] – what it is and how to use it. Short of a Genie, it is the only methodology designed to avert project failure before it occurs.

For more than fifteen years, I've been in the enterprise software implementation field. Let's face it, it's a non-glamorous, complex field aimed at implementing administrative systems for large companies and governments that are looking to automate, and hopefully, improve business functions using technology applications.

Software implementation is actually my second career. My first was a short-lived stint as a grad student working toward a PhD with the goal of becoming a college professor. During the recession of 1992, I was unable to find a job that I was interested in. I was given the opportunity to work as a graduate assistant for the research arm of the University. I was to sell a software package to apparel and textile manufacturers. Despite the fact that the U.S. apparel and textile industry was in decline, I took the job because it was interesting and it allowed me to stay in school while I earned my Master's Degree. Better yet, I could continue to avoid the real world for a couple more years.

Despite my less than stellar academic record as an undergraduate, I found graduate school very interesting because I could apply academic concepts to the practical application of my work with apparel and textile companies. I was pretty good at putting conceptual models together to explain business processes and my work even won a couple of industry sponsored scholarship contests. As I progressed through grad school, when I reached the point where I needed to commit to the PhD program, I realized I didn't like the academic research required to support my models. The research was less about the model itself and more about the statistics supporting the findings. It must have been pretty obvious at the time – I was even pulled aside by a professor who, even though he liked my work, said it was better suited for practitioners.

In 1995, I left graduate school to take a job with Dun & Bradstreet Software as an implementation consultant. The timing was good. Companies were beginning the transition from mainframe green screen systems to relational database technologies with graphical user interfaces or GUIs. Companies were also facing the doomsday scenario known as Y2K. The fact that new technologies – first client server and, soon after, the Internet – were being introduced at a time when organizations needed to make changes to their outdated systems created the perfect storm for the enterprise applications software industry.

The next five years were a roller coaster as we rode the ERP/Y2K wave. Demand for implementation consulting services was so high that consulting firms could not keep up. The technologies were so new that consultants were literally days ahead of the clients in learning the software. The results were mixed: Y2K was averted, but organizations were left with less than optimal systems that weren't properly implemented. Countless papers and articles were written on project success rates and why projects failed. All experts agreed on one thing: surely we have learned our lesson and things will be different moving forward.

I am not so sure about that.

Fast-forward ten years to 2010. The economic downturn and great recession have had significant impact on enterprise systems as many organizations are facing the need to upgrade. While the economy remains in uncertainty, spending on enterprise applications and IT has not changed. Most organizations have halted spending on enterprise business applications, because for the most part, the business can get by with what is in place.

In actuality, the longer an organization waits to upgrade its technology, the more the upgrade will cost. Also, similar to Y2K, several driving external factors are influencing the enterprise software decisions and will likely play a role in your next technology project: consolidation and shared services, software as a service and outsourcing.

Given the economy and other external influencing factors, it is likely that you will have a big project in your future. It may be an application upgrade, a transformation project or a move to an outsourced platform. In any event, it will be complicated. Many organizations are internally integrating systems that cross traditional business functions and externally have more vendor partners involved in technology projects. The result? A complex soup of internal and external project team members, motives and goals.

And here is that pesky statistic again: despite the cumulative knowledge gained from decades of implementing enterprise systems, industry analysts are still predicting that projects have a 70% rate of failure. That means you only have a one in three chance of succeeding.

On closer examination, we really shouldn't be surprised. The reasons that projects fail are the same today as they were ten years ago:

lack of top management commitment, unrealistic expectations, poor requirements definition, improper package selection, gaps between software and business requirements, inadequate resources, underestimating time and cost, poor project management, lack of methodology, underestimating impact of change, lack of training and education, and last, but not least, poor communication.

I can chalk up what happened with Y2K implementations to the fact that we really didn't know what we were doing or to the oppressive deadline that forced things to happen too quickly. But today, we are still seeing 70% failure rates – and if these are caused by the same factors, something is fundamentally wrong.

Fifteen years from now, are we going to look back and wish we had done things differently?

Which brings me back to why I wrote this book. It's about making projects fail-safe. I call it project assurance through collaborative intervention. Project assurance is a disciplined practice developed to deliver projects on time, on-budget, with user acceptance. Collaborative intervention is the breakthrough methodology I have developed and used to obtain project assurance. Collaborative intervention addresses the gaps that lead to the reasons projects fail. Collaborative intervention provides you with a framework and process for closing these gaps.

To some, this collaborative intervention approach may seem overly simplistic – but that may be the point.

Often, we become so engrossed with project status, metrics, and management concerns, that we overlook addressing the root cause of a problem. A problem may be obvious, but the solution, such as increasing top management commitment or changing unrealistic expectations, is not. Let's be honest, collaborative intervention is pretty tricky and relies more on our ability to change and influence human behavior than on our abilities to update a project dashboard or conduct a fit-gap session. It also requires project leadership, not just project management. And, to further complicate things, the leadership may need to come from someone who is not in the position of authority, but who needs to convince the people in positions of authority that change is required for project success.

That's the reason I wrote this book. There is a way and it does work.

No Wishing Required tells a story of business people who are involved in enterprise system implementations. While it is fiction, it is based upon real experiences – good and bad – relating to project management and implementation of enterprise applications technology. This book is both a business documentary of professional growth as well as a cautionary tale for those who don't want to repeat the past in the future. The central characters in this book: Jenny, Bill, and the FirstCorp project team, are fictional. Any resemblance to actual people or events is purely coincidental.

Having said that, I hope you enjoy *No Wishing Required*. If you like this book, please recommend it to a friend or colleague. It is *my wish* that you find value within the concepts of this book and that you do not look back after the next project and say, "I wish I had read Rob's book first."

SECTION 1:

THE BUSINESS CASE FOR A BETTER WAY – PROJECT ASSURANCE

Where is that Genie?

*H*mm ... *when was the last time I saw Bill? Jenny wondered as she backed her car out of the driveway and left for the lunch meeting. It must have been at the go-live party for the last system upgrade at FirstCorp, Jenny thought as she navigated the ever-present traffic on the freeway. That was about two years ago, right before she left FirstCorp to strike out on her own as an independent consultant. That was some go-live party and some upgrade project; there was definitely a lot of pressure to deliver results. However, the upgrade, as difficult as it was, could not compare with original system implementation that started as a disaster and was almost cancelled until Bill Parker stepped in.*

Jenny was surprised to hear from Bill and excited that there might be a consulting opportunity. During the recession, it was tough to stay busy because most organizations, including FirstCorp, had put spending on hold. She anticipated that there would be a lot of opportunities when the economy improves – as there is plenty of pent-up demand.

Driving the six miles to the restaurant, Jenny reflected on her career. She had done the consulting thing with a large firm and a corporate stint at FirstCorp as a project manager. Somehow, these jobs left her unfulfilled. Large scale, ERP projects are complex and experience mixed results. Even if the project is deemed successful, there will always be users who do not like the new system, training issues or perpetual upgrades. It seemed to be a never-ending treadmill.

On the other hand, Jenny enjoyed the challenge associated with the projects, and when the results were realized, which may actually be sometime down the road, it was very rewarding to have been part of the effort. Also, she had learned that there was a better way to assure project success – a lesson learned from Bill Parker.

Bill joined FirstCorp as controller in 1999, just as FirstCorp was getting ready to cut over to a new ERP system in hopes of upgrading its technology and averting the Y2K bug. Bill had just completed a major ERP implementation with his former employer and was looking for a growth opportunity that he hoped to find at FirstCorp.

He had his sights set on the CFO job and beyond. After a few days at FirstCorp, Bill realized that the growth opportunities would never happen unless he got this project on track. Bill was not a systems guy per se, but he understood technology projects and the fact that big projects fail due to poor decisions in the early stages of project lifecycle – the impact of the human factor.

The first time Jenny met Bill Parker was in the bi-weekly executive briefing. She was FirstCorp's project manager and responsible for implementing the financial applications that Bill would be using to run his operations. Needless to say, Jenny was nervous. Hired from a big name consulting firm to lead the system implementation, her life was starting to settle down. Jenny had recently married and wanted to start a family – it was time to get off the road. She had worked on *big implementation projects before, maybe not with this particular ERP application, but how hard could it be?*

Let me tell you ... it is really hard, Jenny said to herself. This project is a disaster. No one seems to be in charge and those who are 'in charge' are indecisive. Cindy, the executive sponsor, is distracted with a new merger/acquisition. The software that was chosen for the implementation will not perform the business functions as promised by the vendors during the vendor selection process. CYA Partners, the consulting firm leading the implementation has implemented this software three times before, but from talking to the consultants on the project – the first two implementations did not go so well. IT is freaking out about the time line and the users are in revolt.

Jenny knew that she was walking into a meeting that was anything but routine. On the agenda was a discussion to change the go-live date, again. Rumors were running rampant that management was going to kill the project. Plus, at this meeting Jenny would meet the new controller, Bill Parker, who had just become her new boss.

Needless to say, Jenny was apprehensive ... and downright worried. She found herself wishing she were back at her old job, on vacation or even out sick. At the moment, the stomach flu sounded appealing. But most of all, she wished that things had been done differently.

Where is that Genie when I need him? Jenny asked herself.

An introduction to *No Wishing Required*

HAVE YOU EVER found yourself in a situation similar to Jenny's? If so, it may be why you're reading this book. I know I've been in situations like this – and more than once. On some occasions, the situation was less dramatic. But occasionally, the situation was arguably worse. There is a silver lining, however, these experiences occurred early enough in my career that I've been able to carry forward the lessons that I learned and embed them within the project assurance practices that this book is about. No one wins all the time, and, if you are resourceful and tenacious, you can learn more from failure than success. Now don't get me wrong, as a consultant I've also been involved in many highly successful projects as well. But the lessons I learned the hard way are the ones that formed a firm foundation for future success.

Over the years, I have been involved in projects of all shapes and sizes ranging from implementing add-on modules to ERP systems to organization-wide transformation projects. I have sat on all sides of the desk: consultant (developer, trainer, project manager, executive partner); customer (technology director); and software vendor (on-site consultant). From each of these vantage points, my goal in this book, *No Wishing Required*, is to give you the insights you need to learn from these experiences and share the tools I've developed to help you navigate the complexities of enterprise project implementations.

Over the last 25 years, advances in technology have provided organizations with software to automate their business functions: finance, human resources, customer relationship management, supply chain management, shop floor control, etc. The purpose of these systems is to make the interaction among internal business processes, customers and suppliers a seamless transaction. However, the selection and implementation of these systems is anything but seamless. In fact, the selection and implementation of these systems is downright complicated. If you work in the business world, you have likely heard or experienced horror stories with enterprise software implementations that range from daily headaches to loss of business. At the end of the day, enterprise technology has changed dramatically during this time, *but human behavior has not.*

In fact, the horror stories continue. Consider the facts that industry experts have recently published:

- IT projects come in at a success rate of only 29%

- Average cost overrun is 56%

- Average schedule delay is 84% beyond plan[1]

Simply translated, this means that nearly 70% of implementations will fail, cost more than 50% over budget, and take nearly twice as long as planned.

The extreme complexity and poor success rate of software implementations continues to baffle many executives. Given that there are accredited bodies of knowledge surrounding software implementations, certifications for project management professionals, a growing field of highly skilled practitioners, endless tools, methodologies and countless studies on what makes projects successful – why do projects still fail? The failures can range from project cost overruns, missed expectations, disgruntled users, to "train wrecks" – which are wastelands of time and money in the form of software that is never implemented or projects that are simply cancelled.

With so many organizations making huge investments of time and money while continuing to experience less than successful outcomes with these large-scale projects, I began to ask myself, *what if there was a way to assure project success – or at minimum, increase the odds of success?* To address this question, I investigated the history of why software implementation projects fail. Combining my research with personal experience, I realized that failure is avoidable. Armed with this certainty, I developed a fail-safe process for managing projects to success by addressing failure before it occurs.

On becoming an advocate

A S MY ROLE advanced from project manager to project executive, my responsibilities changed from hands-on project management to project assurance advocacy –

making sure that projects were delivered on time, on-budget with client acceptance. In doing so, I found a need to translate tactical project management methodology – developed for the tactical role of the project manager – to the strategic perspective of a project executive or executive sponsor. The translation was required because as a project executive, I could only spend a short periods of time with different project teams, therefore, I had to be more efficient. At any given moment, I had to know **when** to conduct an assessment of the project, **what** to look for at each point in time, and **how** to intervene if the project was not on track.

To accomplish these goals, I developed the project assurance methodology known as ***collaborative intervention***[SM]. Collaborative intervention is a project assurance methodology designed to align project expectations, resources and scope with the goal of increasing the project's probability of success. Collaborative intervention is different from other project management methodologies in that it addresses key project failure points before they occur by creating a collaborative environment comprised of key project stakeholders to discuss and resolve project issues and roadblocks before they arise.

Using the principles of collaborative intervention, I was able to maintain a high success rate for our projects – so successful, in fact, that our clients began asking for project assurance services for other projects in their organization. Interestingly enough, these were projects that were not within our capabilities or were too large for our firm to handle. But the results speak for themselves. Regardless of the scope, type or size of the implementation, collaborative intervention works as well as any insurance policy you could buy!

Within the pages of No Wishing Required, you will find the answers to conducting project assessments and interventions designed to ensure your project targets are well within scope. You will gain working knowledge as to when to conduct point in time assessments, what the best practices are for each phase of the software implementation lifecycle, and workable tools, tips and techniques for conducting an intervention to get a project back on track.

I'm excited about the sharing power of project assurance through collaborative intervention. At the end of the day, I know what's worked for me can work for you.

The executive committee meeting

Jenny straightened her shoulders and walked into the executive committee meeting. She took her seat and, once again, wished she were on a far away island. Seated around the conference room table were the executive team members whom she thought could not be more clichéd:

Bill – the new FirstCorp Controller, and Jenny's new boss

Brett – the stubborn IT Director who always sat with his arms crossed while demanding that business requirements be defined for every request

Mary – the overly nice, HR VP who was always smiling and seemed out of place during the technical discussions, but was willing to negotiate solutions

Bobby – the well-dressed executive partner from Coleman, Young and Alexander, LLP, (a.k.a. CYA Partners) the systems integration consulting firm, a man who always appeared tan and rested - which was at odds his habit of dozing off during meetings

Joining Jenny on the project management team:

Tim – Jenny's counterpart and the project manager from CYA Partners, Tim is well intentioned and competent, but a bit hamstrung by the inexperience of the consultants assigned to the project

Janice – the charming change management and education lead. Janice had been the project manager for several past projects and was close to retiring. Since she was having a hard time grasping the complexities of the new systems, she was assigned to lead the change management and training effort for lack of other qualified candidates. Jenny was brought in to replace Janice as overall project manager. She didn't hold this against her, though, and actually took Jenny under her wing for guidance when she could. In all actuality, she just wanted to retire.

And absent again today:

Cindy – the COO and executive sponsor. Bill, Brett and Mary all reported to Cindy and at the end of the day, Cindy had the final word and everybody knew it. Nothing could get done without Cindy's approval – which wasn't hard to get if she could be found. Cindy was leading the integration of FirstCorp's latest acquisition and as a result, Cindy is absent again today.

Jenny wondered if anything would change because Bill was now in their midst, but it quickly became apparent that was not to be the case. As usual, Tim began the meeting by jumping right into the status report and issues log as if we were continuing a previous meeting. The finger pointing started immediately as Tim mentioned that IT was behind schedule on development. Brett reacted by crossing his arms and proclaiming that IT was behind due to the fact that the business side kept changing the systems requirements.

"Here we go, again ... " Jenny muttered.

"We keep changing the requirements because the BusinessWare software is not functioning as promised and the consultants lacked the knowledge to conduct a proper fit-gap analysis," Tim replied, looking to Bobby (who was starting to nod off) for support.

The discussion lobbied back and forth for another five minutes when Bill stepped in. "So what is BusinessWare's position on this, Jenny?" he said.

"BusinessWare's position is that the system is functioning as designed and they have asked us to log a case. I wish it was a better situation – but apparently we're stuck in tech support hell," Jenny replied.

"Have we escalated the issues? Where is our account manager?" Bill inquired.

"Probably on the golf course," replied Brett, as Bill looked at him in confusion, while everyone else chuckled.

"No I'm serious," Brett clarified, "we don't see too much of our account manager except when he occasionally drops by to take Cindy to lunch or the other executives golfing at the country club."

"I have been getting some voice messages from BusinessWare, but it's never the same person," Janice added. "I'm not even sure why they are calling me."

"Look," Bill responded. "I know I'm new here and a lot has happened to get us to this point and that there are questions as to whether this project should even continue. Well, the bottom line is this: FirstCorp has invested a great amount of time and effort into this implementation and is realizing that the project will not bring the anticipated returns. However, we may be too far down the road to turn back and be able to recover. Given the imminent merger, if this project does not succeed, we may need to clean house. If we can't get this software implementation back on track, all of our positions here are in jeopardy."

Bill continued. "Because I have some history with projects like this, Cindy has asked me to intervene. For the next two weeks, the executive committee is putting the project on hold while we take a closer look at where the project is in the implementation lifecycle, conduct an assessment and determine if and how to get it restarted successfully."

"I will be holding a meeting at 8:00 a.m. tomorrow morning to set expectations for the assessment," Bill stated, adding, "meeting adjourned – and for God's sake, somebody wake up Bobby!"

"Jenny, can you please stick around for a few minutes? I need to speak with you," asked Bill.

Jenny slowly closed her project notebook. "Sure, Bill. I'm wishing for a way to make this project succeed."

"No wishing required, Jenny," Bill grinned. "Let me show you exactly what I mean by intervention."

Assessing the point in time

"Jenny, I bet this isn't the way you envisioned meeting your new manager," Bill said, after everyone else left the room.

"No, not exactly," she replied. "You know I've only been here at FirstCorp for six months myself."

"Yes, I know. You have a good reputation here, and I need your observations to help me figure out how we got into this situation," Bill observed. "I've talked with some of members of the executive team and they are legitimately concerned about the health of this project and our ability to successfully implement the systems."

"Honestly, I'm concerned, too. We've all been wishing for the proverbial decoder ring to decipher what is really happening in the project," explained Jenny. "We've been running on gut feel which makes it hard to communicate to the executive committee. As it is, they won't even make a decision unless Cindy is present. And she is never here. It makes everyone feel that she doesn't care."

"Oh she cares alright," Bill quickly said. "However, she is consumed with the merger and the CEO has said that is her top priority. That's why she asked me to step in."

"That makes sense," Jenny responded. "So how can I help?"

"Since you are fairly new to the project, you don't have the history and battle scars that Mary, Brett and Janice have," Bill explained, "I need you to give me an update of where we are in the project."

"Sure, no problem. We're about to finish the development phase and begin testing," Jenny said.

Bill thought for a moment. "So if things were going according to plan, we would be getting testing and training ramped up to test defects and to start the process to gain user acceptance through testing, training and communications, right?"

"Exactly," responded Jenny. "But that isn't the case. I've been thinking about this non-stop lately, trying to figure out how we got to this point."

"So what is your prognosis, Jenny?"

"I think we've made mistakes from the very beginning," Jenny related. "Instead of properly defining all of the requirements, we decided we needed a new system for general ledger, accounts payable and purchasing because our current home-grown system was not Y2K compliant. We did requirements analysis just for those modules and came up with a budget."

"Well, it sounds like things got started on the right track ..." Bill began when Jenny interrupted him.

"I agree, but please remember, I hadn't joined the project team yet," Jenny reminded him.

"OK got it," grinned Bill. "Please continue, Jenny. Remember, I'm not here to evaluate your performance, I just need to know how we got into this situation."

"Fair enough," Jenny took a deep breath and jumped in. "From what I can tell, the project team had a good methodical process for the first three financial modules, but then things started unraveling."

"First, the billing department got involved because they needed a new system to track and bill for project costs, so the team figured as long as we were buying a financial package, then the billing and project costing modules should be added to the mix," Jenny said. "After a discovery session with billing, it was realized that a lot of the information needed for project costing to feed billing was in our time entry and payroll systems, which also needed to be upgraded along with the rest of the HR applications for personnel and benefits tracking. However, time was slipping away and we failed to do our due diligence for the other modules because we figured if we purchased software from one of the leading ERP vendors, they would have this functionality covered. So in the end, we just increased our project budget to cover the additional costs."

"Did the time line change?" Bill questioned.

"Kinda, but we still need to beat the Y2K deadline," Jenny answered.

"OK, so what happened next?" asked Bill.

Jenny went on. "Each group went back to write up their requirements and we scheduled the vendor demonstrations. Under pressure to meet our time line, we did not have all of the requirements when the vendors came in. So we went through the demonstration and picked the software we liked the best – the BusinessWare modules – based on what we knew. A few other firms in our industry use BusinessWare software packages and those references checked out, so the team figured the risk was minimal."

"How did you choose the integrator," Bill inquired, "and what is the deal with that narcoleptic Bobby?"

Jenny smiled. "Bobby lives next door to Ted, the CEO, so that should tell you a few things," she explained. "His firm, CYA Partners, has done a number of projects with FirstCorp, so they know our business. In addition, BusinessWare provided a list of three system integrators – and CYA Partners was on the list. We got proposals from the other two firms, but let's be honest about it: Bobby's firm had the inside track and won the business."

"So how are they doing?" Bill looked up from his rapidly expanding notes.

"OK," Jenny spoke slowly. "Not everything is their fault. They have some good people and some not so good people. On the downside, they don't have enough knowledge of the BusinessWare software, but this stuff is so new I'm not sure anybody does. On the upside, they are responsive to our request if a team member is not working out and they will not hesitate to tell us when the project is behind schedule because of items we are responsible for."

"Hence the friction between Tim and Brett," Bill observed.

"Exactly," Jenny said.

Bill pushed back his chair from the conference room table and began to pace the room.

"So let me summarize what you've shared with me to make sure I understand the situation," he began. "First, before the official implementation began, the requirements were not properly defined. Next, the software and services procurements were loose, so we're not even sure we have the right packages. Thirdly, there are going to be gaps between the software capabilities and the business requirements, the extent of which we are starting to realize six months later, and finally, we aren't sure we allocated enough time, resources and money to the project in the first place."

Jenny nodded. "Yep, that pretty much sums it up."

"OK, so was it about this time that you joined the project team?" Bill queried.

"Yes, I came on board right after all the contracts were signed and started the planning phase, " Jenny explained. "Tim was on board as well and together we developed the project charter and detailed project plan. Given the procurement processes, I found several gaps mainly in the area of change management and training. Since we didn't have the budget to pay the consultants for this piece of the project, we decided to do it in-house and assigned Janice as the project manager for the change management area."

"Does she have any experience in change management and training?" Bill asked.

"Some experience from her past projects," responded Jenny. "But I am not sure she – or the rest of the team, for that matter – fully understood the magnitude of the changes until we completed the design phase. Janice is a good project manager and can get things done if she has the right people. I guess we just aren't sure that she does."

"So you finished planning, closed some gaps between the statement of work and project plan and began development, right?" Bill asked.

"Right," Jenny said, "except IT could not stabilize the demonstration environment in time for the design session. It was a comedy of errors. We couldn't get connectivity to the new servers in the conference room. Brett had to step in and stabilize the environment, but not before we lost two weeks in the process."

Jenny continued. "And it only escalated from there. Once we started the design sessions, some sessions went well and others were like opening Pandora's Box. We began to realize that we had never defined business requirements before and we had built our processes around the previous system. Since we needed to continue to define requirements we did not anticipate, we had to schedule additional meetings extending the design phase. To make matters worse, the extension was during the HR Benefits open enrollment period. Because of this conflict, we weren't sure we had the right people from HR involved. I think this will probably come back to haunt us during testing."

"It probably will," Bill said. "OK, Jenny. I think that's enough for today. I have to give Cindy an update this afternoon and I'm starting to get a headache. I want to thank you for the input and your candor. I'll see you bright and early tomorrow morning."

As she left the conference room, Jenny didn't know what to think. Did I say too much, too little? Did I throw people under the bus? I can't tell. I actually have a headache too, hey … maybe it will turn into a stomach virus and I can miss the 8:00 a.m. meeting!

"I know, I know, just wishful thinking," she said, out loud, to no one in particular.

The expectations meeting

Well, it's 8:00 a.m. and no stomach virus, Jenny thought to herself. Guess I'm going to have to gut it out and sit through this meeting. Given the gravity of the situation, she noticed that everybody else had also arrived early – including Bobby who was armed with an extra large coffee. Everyone apprehensively took a seat around Bill's conference table overlooking the FirstCorp campus.

"I think everyone knows why we're here today," Bill began. "As I mentioned yesterday, Cindy asked me to step in and assess the current situation and to determine a plan to get the project back on track. I've already spoken with many of you informally. As a result, I know that there are many reasons we are in this situation – some of which may be beyond your control."

"Here's what will happen next," Bill continued. "Over the next ten days we'll be conducting a project assessment and, if necessary, an intervention. Jenny and I will be leading this process. Our goal is to present the assessment findings to Cindy next Friday. We'll begin this process by reviewing the relevant project documentation and cross-referencing it to make sure we have covered all the gaps. In addition, we'll meet with each of you individually to get your input on the situation and ideas for potential solutions. From these documentation reviews and one-on-one interviews, we'll generate our recommendations."

"Any questions?" Bill looked around the group. His question was met with silence. Someone coughed.

"OK, starting with the action items," Bill went down his list. "Tim and Jenny, I will need a copy of the following documents: the original needs assessment, the project strategy, the budget, the RFP for software and services, the vendor proposal, the project charter, the detail project plan, the statement of work, the project issues log, the risk plan and system design documents."

"In addition, I'll be contacting each of you for interviews to get your input, perceptions and suggestions," Bill said. "Thanks, everyone. And Jenny, I'll see you in my office at 1:00 p.m. to get started."

"Can you believe this guy?" Tim said as we walked out of the room. "I know he is new, but he doesn't have a clue how things get done around here."

"You know, Tim, I think I'm going to give him the benefit of the doubt," Jenny said.

"Obviously, you have to," Tim replied. "He is your manager. But frankly, I just don't get it – we just completed the project audit from that third party firm. Wasn't that enough?"

"I don't know Tim," she replied. "In all actuality, the audit only looked at our project management methodology. As a result, we tightened a few things up in terms of status reporting and project governance, but the audit didn't address the other issues we are having with the software or change impact. There was no root cause analysis."

"Well, even if we do address the root cause, it's not like Cindy is going to make any changes," Tim challenged. "We all know how she is."

"We'll find out, won't we, Tim?" Jenny glanced at her watch. "Let's just get started on pulling the documents together that Bill requested. It's looking like I've got some long days ahead of me."

The documentation review

" **I** believe this is everything," Jenny said as she piled the last stack of documents on the conference table in Bill's office.

"Great," Bill grinned as he pressed the button on the coffeemaker. "Coffee is brewing, let's get started."

For the next five hours and four cups of coffee, Bill and Jenny poured through various project documentation from the first four phases of the project – strategy, acquisition, planning and design. Finally, at 5:00 p.m. they wrapped up.

"Let's regroup early tomorrow morning," Bill said. "Is 7:00 a.m. good for you?"

Jenny nodded, sending her husband a text message alerting him to her early morning schedule.

As she drove home, Jenny realized that listening to her favorite classical station was not as soothing as usual. In fact, she found herself gripping the steering wheel so hard that her fingers hurt. She couldn't help but think there had to be a better way. After all, she had completed her project management certification last year. This type of project derailment was not supposed to happen on her watch. Granted, she was not involved in the strategy and selection process, but she should have seen some of the warning signs as we developed the project charter and work plan. "Don't beat yourself up too much, Jenny," she said to herself as she pulled into the driveway.

It was a beautiful, crisp fall evening, so Jenny decided to go for a run to clear her head.

As she began her usual three-mile loop, she realized that her pent-up stress was making her run way too fast. She decided to slow her pace or the run would quickly become a short run and frustrating walk home if she didn't. As her thoughts drifted back to the conversation with Bill from the previous day when she was giving him the project update, it hit her like a ton of bricks. "We know what we have to do, but not necessarily how to do it!" She exclaimed. Wait a second, did I really say that? It sounds like one of those overly simplified clichés developed by some consultant writing a how-to book – we know what we have to do, but not how to do it.

In fact, Jenny realized, it was true. Once the train left the station, everyone felt it was too late to address the issues for fear of personal or team failure. They were so focused on making the date that they rushed through the procurement process. They thought there were going to be gaps in the software, but didn't know how to address them. They knew that they needed BusinessWare to step up and resolve their critical issues, but they couldn't get the issues escalated. They knew that Cindy made all the decisions, but not how to get the issues in front of her. And, they subconsciously knew that there were potential time bombs waiting to explode. When the bombs eventually did explode in the form of the project being placed on hold, their collective fate was placed in this assessment.

As Jenny rounded the final corner and headed down the hill toward her house, she felt a little better. Bill was providing an objective opinion and identifying the real issues. The main question: could he execute the solution?

Carbs, caffeine and clarity

She stopped at the donut shop and picked up a couple of bagels.

"Nothing like a few carbs to go with caffeine," she said to Bill, running into him in the elevator on the way to his office at 7:00 a.m. the next morning.

Bill chuckled. "Make that a double – I brought donuts, too." So much for calorie containment, Jenny thought. Good thing she had gone for a run last night.

Bill and Jenny continued the document review throughout the day, making copious notes and identifying key issues on the white board. At the end of the second day, they had identified several themes.

1. Not everything was a disaster. We have some good people on the project team and we have a sound project management methodology and structure. We did a good job of defining the requirements for the core financial modules, which was the

original scope of the project. The related project tracks or 'swim lanes' are progressing with few issues.

2. *Our expectations and time line were flawed from the beginning. We not only underestimated the effort and complexity of the procurement process and contract negotiations, but also how long it would take to get our development environment for the design sessions in place. We painted the IT department into a corner to get us a development environment and, because they underestimated the effort as well, they committed to an unrealistic timeline. In addition, the early phases of the project went past their completion date, yet we did not change the target go-live date.*

3. *The project team was stretched too thin. Proficient team members were involved in every meeting while having to continue to do their full time jobs. Worse still, several of the people who were assigned to the project were not competent. They were offered to the project team because some of the operations managers did not want to give up their best people to the project.*

4. *We kept a good log of the issues. We just weren't able to get resolution to the issues either internally or externally. Internally, we presented our concerns and risks about the target date, lack of proper requirements, and misaligned project team members on several occasions to the executive committee, but with Cindy's lack of participation, there was a reluctance to act. Externally, we seemed to have no visibility with BusinessWare. You would think that because FirstCorp is a large, well-known company, the vendor would be concerned if we could not implement the software. The impact of bad press would be devastating to BusinessWare. In fact, there were several show stopper defects within the financial modules that would need resolution if the software was to be implemented.*

5. *Some of the software modules were definitely off track and behind schedule. HR was pulled into the project without the opportunity to think through their requirements. It appears that FirstCorp's business process and employee environment are a complex mix of unions, multi-national employees, hourly, part time and salaried employees – each with their own benefit mix and payroll schedule.*

"So what do you think?" Bill asked, at the end of the second, long afternoon.

"Frankly, I wish we had gone through this exercise sooner," Jenny responded. "On one hand, we probably could have prevented some of these issues before they occurred. Looking back, there definitely were some critical points in time that, if we had done an earlier assessment of the project, we'd be in better shape now. On the other hand, even if we had done the assessment, I'm not sure we had the structure and consensus to implement any changes. But one thing I do know is that everything is becoming a lot clearer now."

"I agree," Bill said. "Let's schedule the interviews with the other team members."

"Let's start with interviewing Brett," Jenny said. "To me, he seems the most skeptical."

The interviews

Brett's office was tucked away in the back corner of the IT Department overlooking the parking lot. Brett was a portly guy who preferred short sleeve shirts and enjoyed fishing. His office walls were lined with striped bass and trout mounted on wooden plaques. A gleaming brass trophy of a large catfish served as a hat-rack for an Atlanta Braves baseball cap. Brett was not really happy with the project, but that was no surprise as he wasn't really happy with most things at FirstCorp. In his defense, IT did get a lot of requests dumped on them – always a crisis and at the last minute – and never a lot of thanks.

It was easy to see that Brett was increasingly becoming fed up with the constant requests from the project team —for greater access/security, data refreshes or more development environment.

"Tim and I have done our best to limit these requests," Jenny mentioned to Bill as they walked down the hallway to Brett's office. "But some were necessary, essentially always putting us at odds with Brett."

Once seated in Brett's office, Bill began the interview by asking Brett to provide his take on the project up to this point.

Despite the occasional profanities, Brett was conflicted. "I recognize that a lot of work has gone into the project up to this point and that the some of the delays were a result of my people having to react to constant requests without really understanding the priority of the requests," Brett answered. "I'm OK with the progress being made with the financial applications, but the HR side is a damn mess - struggling with requirements and constantly sending mixed signals."

"To tell you the truth, I think the bigger issue is that BusinessWare isn't listening – or if they are, they aren't taking us seriously," Brett was becoming increasingly agitated. "My concern is fundamentally about the lack of response from BusinessWare. My suggestion is that I call Charles, the BusinessWare account manager, to set up a meeting or at least a conference call as part of this assessment."

Immediately Bill and Jenny agreed. They both knew that many of the outstanding issues could not be resolved without vendor support.

"Look, I know my job is on the line here," Brett stated flatly. "But I am convinced that the entire scope of the project cannot be implemented by the date scheduled. And I'll be honest with you, Bill, I'm skeptical of your ability to convince Cindy to take the recommendations of yet another assessment seriously."

Overall, Brett made it clear that he felt that FirstCorp had bitten off more than it could chew. However, Brett concluded by saying that while IT was supportive of the project; he wanted to make sure that the proposed solutions were realistic and implementable within the project timeframe. Bill promised to review the assessment results and recommendations with Brett before meeting with Cindy. This made Brett feel a little better.

The next interview was with Mary from Human Resources. Mary's office was warm, inviting and well decorated. It felt like a visit to her living room. Throughout her office were pictures of her family as well as posters and mugs from FirstCorp's HR recruiting campaigns.

When Bill and Jenny arrived, her two direct reports and the corporate counsel were in her office discussing a personnel issue in one of the plants. It did not sound good – people were going to have to be let go and they were anticipating potential lawsuits and press involvement.

They waited outside her office for at least 15 minutes, until the door opened and Mary appeared.

"Mary, we can reschedule for a better time," said Bill.

"I doubt there will be a better time," quipped Mary. The usually cheerful and reassuring Mary was not here today; instead they met with the stern Mary, VP of HR, who was obviously stressed with the latest personnel crisis and not really happy with the software project.

She didn't really want to have to deal with Jenny and Bill right now, but did not want to reschedule. Plus, she needed someone to take her frustrations out on.

"So Jenny, what's the latest with the software issues from the vendor?" Mary began the interview on the offensive. "And has Brett figured out those technical issues yet?"

"We're working on that, Mary," Jenny smiled in reply.

"You know what? Cindy is just going to cancel this project and we are going to go onto the systems from our acquisition of Parnew," Mary challenged as she looked at Bill. "And in all actuality, it might not be such a bad idea. Parnew implemented a new HR system last year and it appears to be light years ahead of where we are. I'm not even sure why you both are wasting two weeks with this assessment."

"If you remember, Cindy has asked me to go through this process," Bill replied easily.

"Exactly, so that she has what she needs to stop this train wreck!" Mary shot back.

Jenny felt her stomach sink and heart rate jump as the interview continued. She could see Mary's assistant poking her head in trying to get Mary's attention, the division manager was on the phone.

"Well, I did speak with Cindy about the systems from the new company. Yes, they have some solutions in place, but not for all the modules we need. Our business is more complex than Parnew's in several significant areas," Bill countered.

"Who planned this project anyway? Who plans design sessions in the middle of open enrollment?" Mary paced the room, arms folded. "Our existing systems are getting the job done, so why are we involved in this project?"

"OK, I understand," said Bill.

"Look, that's all I have to say," Mary strode to the door and opened it. "I've got to deal with this other crisis right now."

"I thought that went rather well," Bill mused, as they left the HR department.

"Yeah, right," Jenny responded. "Mary's not usually wound this tightly. I think she feels dragged into this project and obviously she's dealing with some heavy personnel issues."

Next up on the interview circuit were the project consultants from CYA Partners. Bill and Jenny were anticipating some defensiveness – and they weren't disappointed. They met Bobby and Tim for lunch in the company cafeteria.

Both men were defensive of their position and tried to put blame back on the FirstCorp project team. Obviously, they didn't want to admit fault, because CYA may then have to provide additional services on their dime to cover their insufficiencies. Or even worse, give FirstCorp a refund.

Tim pointed out that there weren't enough resources – or even the right resources – assigned to the project team. Bobby mentioned change management and training and offered to provide additional services for those areas. Funny, Jenny noticed Bobby always seemed to be about additional services.

Jenny did ask about a couple of CYA consultants who led the team astray in several areas of the project. She believed that they might not have possessed the level of experience that the firm originally proposed. She reminded them of their young consultant who didn't fully understand the difference between debits and credits and always got the plus and minus signs confused. And then there was the example of the consultants who were attending training for their assigned software modules after the fit-gap occurred. Saving the best for last, Jenny brought up their consultant who e-mailed the high resolution picture of his boat with the subject line 'For Sale' to the entire company – nearly crippling FirstCorp's e-mail server.

"OK," Tim acknowledged. "Maybe we are partially to blame for the situation." Bobby looked down at his empty plate.

"We really do want to make sure you succeed," Bobby admitted. "I know you joke that we get a lot of business because I'm Ted's neighbor, but you guys know Ted and his temper. It's not unusual for him to show up after work at my house when things aren't going well and rip me a new one – even while my kids are playing video games in the next room. So tell me, how do you want to proceed?"

"Let us finish our process and make some initial recommendations," Bill said. "We'll meet with you again before talking to Cindy."

"In the meantime, I'm going to call Charles at the software company and make sure he knows what is going on here," interjected Bobby. "I don't think we can fix some of these functionality issues without him."

"I'd appreciate that," said Bill. "You should know that Brett is going to call him as well and suggest a meeting or conference call."

"I will do the same, Bill," Bobby grinned. "I think once Charles knows the situation, we will have his support."

The final interview was with Janice. A FirstCorp veteran, Janice had managed countless projects in the past, some good, some bad, but none as large or complicated as this project. She was the initial project manager for the strategy and acquisition phase and, frankly, was in way over her head. She had even told Jenny that this project was going to be her swan song into retirement, but it was turning out to be more of a holding cell.

In many ways, Janice represented the old guard – slow to grasp new concepts, but too valuable in organizational knowledge to be cast aside. When Tim and Jenny reported to the executive committee that they needed a change management and training lead, Janice was immediately selected. Looking back, it was clearly a decision made as a solution for what to do with Janice rather than one based on her qualifications for the change management job.

The interview with Janice was actually more of a monologue. She gave Bill and Jenny endless history lessons as to why things will never change as well as countless stories of the good old days at FirstCorp. On her office walls hung the proof – probably more than one hundred photos of Janice with every CEO and every major function that the company had for the last 35 years.

Thirty minutes later, Janice paused. "You know, to be honest I really don't know much about change management and training, but I'm glad to be involved in the project," she said. "You won't find anyone else on the project team who is as loyal to FirstCorp as I am – it's just that this isn't the way I envisioned my career ending."

"Wowser," Bill said after the interview. "Janice really does have a lot of good experience. Obviously she is in the wrong position. I wish we could find a better way to use her skills."

"Me, too," Jenny replied sadly. "So what's next?"

They walked through FirstCorp's hallways back to their offices. "Let's have the conference call with BusinessWare," Bill said, "and then meet to discuss our findings."

When Jenny got back to her office, she found an e-mail from Brett inviting Bill and her to a conference call with Charles from Business-Ware. She forwarded the invite to Bobby and Tim so that they could all participate. The conference call was scheduled for 10:00 a.m. the next day in Brett's office.

The conference call

"**H**ello, Charles, are you there?" Brett pulled the conference call speaker closer.

"I'm here," Charles' voice crackled through the receiver, as Brett tapped on the volume button.

"Good," responded Brett. "I have Jenny, our project manager, Bobby and Tim from CYA Partners, and Bill, who is our new controller, on the line with me."

"OK, morning everyone. Bill, nice to meet you," Charles said. "Will Janice be joining us as well?"

"Thanks," Bill replied curiously, "no, Janice won't be joining us."

"OK then, on my side, I have asked Lisa to join us. Lisa is our new client executive assigned to FirstCorp," Charles started.

"Welcome Lisa," Brett replied. "Charles, you just said that she is our new client executive, but I wasn't aware that we even had a client executive. We thought you were the account manager."

"Well, in a sense, I am the account manager, but I actually handle more of the sales side," Charles explained. "Lisa handles the day-to-day issues."

"Charles, this is Jenny talking. Did we have a client executive before Lisa?" she asked.

"Well, actually this is a little embarrassing," Charles said, clearing his throat, *"but as it turns out we have had a lot of turn-over and re-orgs at our company. Originally, you had Mike as your client manager, then Francis and then George."*

"I have to say I'm a little shocked," Jenny responded. *"Why is it we've never met with these people?"*

Charles quickly replied, *"I'm not sure how that can be – they've been in contact with Janice all along."*

"Janice isn't the project manager," Bill stated.

"Well, if she's not, then who is?" Charles quizzed.

"Jenny is our project manager," Bill clarified. *"She took over from Janice after the contract was signed."*

Silence.

"Guess it's a good thing I'm new and that we are having this conversation," said Lisa, breaking the silence. *"At least we have a clean slate to start working with."*

"Yes, it definitely is a good thing," Jenny said, as everyone laughed nervously.

"Well, now that we've gotten the account manager relationships straightened out, what's up?" Charles asked.

"Go ahead, Bill," Brett said.

"Charles, we are having some issues with your software," Bill explained. *"We're trying to get a handle on exactly how many problems exist, but according to Jenny and Tim, there are several show stoppers."*

"Have you logged them with our Tech Support?" Lisa asked.

"Of course," Jenny replied, *"but we aren't getting any resolution. And now Tech Support is telling us that the issues will be resolved in a future release. Frankly, we can't afford to wait. As Bill mentioned, there are a couple of show stoppers in there."*

"Well, this isn't good news," said Charles. *"Lisa, how can you help FirstCorp with this?"*

"Jenny, if you can get me a prioritized list of your issues with the corresponding case number, I will see that these issues get properly escalated," Lisa said. "And we can have a daily call between us until the most critical issues get resolved."

"Works for me," Jenny said, deeply relieved on a couple of fronts.

"Let me tell you that I'm glad to hear that you are going to help us resolve these issues, Charles," Bill said. "But there's one more thing that you need to know. Cindy has asked me to conduct an assessment of the project to determine if we will keep moving forward with the implementation. We are presenting our findings to her next Friday. We need to make progress on this list before then. I also think it would be good for you to be at the meeting as well."

"Got it," said Charles. "We will make the issues a priority here at BusinessWare and we'll also will be at the meeting next Friday. And please know that we're sorry for the confusion about Janice – we really thought she was your project manager."

"Jenny," interjected Lisa, "send me that list ASAP."

"Will do."

"OK," Bill said in closing. "We'll let Jenny and Lisa take it from here. Charles, we'll contact you with the meeting details once we have them."

"Sounds good. Talk to you later," Charles said, as he signed off the call.

"Can you believe that?" Tim asked incredulously. "We've had a client executive the whole time, but they were talking to the wrong person. Unbelievable!"

"Brett, thanks for setting this call up, it was obviously very helpful," Bill said.

"Yeah, thanks," Bobby chimed in. "So what happens next?" he asked, turning to Bill.

Bill thought a moment. "Jenny and I are going to get together to summarize our findings. Then we'll have a meeting to discuss them as well as our preliminary recommendations before going to Cindy. I'll send you an invite once we can finalize a time."

Why projects fail

You would think that, over the years, project management would have evolved along with the technology that is being implemented. In truth, the high rate of project failure in today's organizations is proof that project implementation methodologies have not kept pace.

So, why do projects fail?

1. Lack of top management commitment

2. Unrealistic expectations

3. Poor requirements definition

4. Improper package selection

5. Gaps between software and business requirements

6. Inadequate resources

7. Underestimating time and cost

8. Poor project management / lack of methodology

9. Underestimating impact of change

10. Lack of training / education

Look closely – you may be surprised to see that a common denominator is not technology, but people.

Their decisions, expectations, and actions are the key components in project success – and failure. When I worked on PeopleSoft implementations, I was often quoted saying, "If you took the People out of a PeopleSoft project, it would be easy to implement." Why? Because for the most part, software is coded to perform a function, but people and/or the project team members are required to develop the plan, evaluate systems and services, manage the implementation, design and configure the application, test the system, train the users and communicate the change to the organization.

In tandem, consider the evolution of project management methodologies.

Standard methodology for software implementation

TODAY'S SOFTWARE IMPLEMENTATION methodology is adopted from the Waterfall Model used by the manufacturing and construction industries. The waterfall model is a sequential implementation process where each phase follows a previous phase flowing steadily downward like a waterfall.

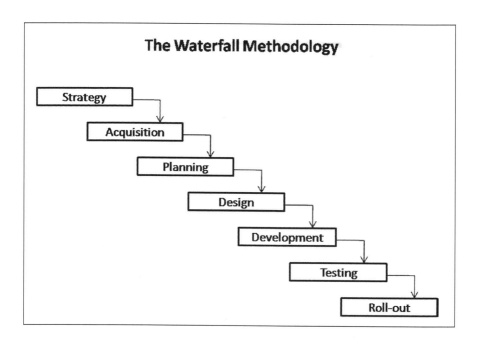

Since no formal methodology was available at the time of the first enterprise system implementations, the waterfall model has become the de facto methodology used by companies and systems integrators. Over the years, it has evolved to account for ongoing project activities such as project management and change management.

The waterfall methodology is the most structured of the methods, stepping through requirements, analysis, design, coding, and testing in a strict, pre-planned, "all at once" sequence. Progress is often measured in terms of deliverable artifacts: requirement specifications, design documents, test plans, code reviews and the like.

A common criticism of the waterfall model is its inflexible division of a project into separate stages, where commitments are made early on, making it difficult to react to changes in requirements as the project executes. This means that the waterfall model is likely to be unsuitable if requirements are not well understood/defined or changed in the course of the project.[2]

Inflexible, archaic project management methodologies can result in significant cost overruns as well as failure to meet the fundamental business requirements of the software implementation over the course of the project. After the purchase, the most significant cost occurs during the development phase. If, during the strategy phase, there are gaps in the business requirements and the implementation plan − it could spell disaster for the implementation itself.

To head off disaster before it occurs, I decided to map the reasons that projects fail to the timed phases of a software implementation. What I found was intriguing: although failure points are present throughout the project lifecycle, *most, if not all, can occur before the project technically begins.*

Reasons Project Fail	Strategy	Acquisition	Planning	Design	Development	Testing	Roll-out
1. Lack of Top Mgt. Commitment	X	X	X	X	X	X	X
2. Unrealistic Expectations	X	X	X	X	X	X	
3. Poor Requirements Definition	X	X		X			
4. Improper Package Selection		X					
5. Gaps between software and requirements		X		X			
6. Inadequate Resources			X	X	X	X	
7. Underestimating Time and Costs			X	X	X		
8. Poor Project Management			X	X	X	X	
9. Underestimating Impact of Change			X		X		X
10. Lack of Training / Education			X		X	X	X

To combat early failure, software implementation needs project assurance from the beginning.

Reliance on tools and templates

THE TOP REASONS that projects fail really haven't changed. The reality is that most project teams are aware of why projects fail, but don't know how to address the reasons. Instead, most project managers look to 'tools' or 'templates' to guide them. I've seen countless documents and spreadsheets for requirements gathering and mapping, tracking users' skills and training needs, and even stakeholder analysis and involvements. The problem is not the lack of tools, it's a lack of understanding and review of the content of those tools. Yes, tools and templates provide a structure for content, but the content itself is gathered and evaluated by the project team.

In addition to tools and templates, people today expect software to solve problems for them. In fact, I even hesitated using the term 'collaborative' intervention because 'collaborative' is the connotation today for collaborative software. Collaborative software is both a blessing and a curse. It is a blessing in terms of its ability to share project documents, collect online feedback and provide project workspaces. It is a curse in that it doesn't address the reasons projects fail or create the environment for their resolution. If a project is off track and needs an intervention, that intervention needs to happen in person. Why? Some of the issues that may be discussed will be too sensitive for an impersonal online discussion. Chat sessions are not the best way to resolve complex business problems. There is a need for personal interaction: the need to observe facial expressions, have eye contact and observe body language and voice tone in order to get full information from all dimensions.

Ensuring project success requires doing what is obvious, but not easy. In fact, that's why I've titled this book *No Wishing Required*. You simply can't wish away problems; you need to confront and resolve them before they become insurmountable.

I can't count the number of times that project team members or project managers have brought issues to my attention that require a conversation with another team member. My first questions is always "Have you talked with so and so?" and nine times out of ten, the answer is, "No, but we exchanged some e-mails." After evaluating the e-mail chain, there is usually both miscommunication and misunderstanding as the culprits. Project team members can hide behind e-mails and other collaborative software packages to avoid the issue. No matter how much technology exists to manage projects with online communication packages (with the exception of video conferencing) complex project issues need to be resolved with a face-to-face discussion.

I was involved in a situation where senior executives responsible for different business functions (IT, HR and Finance) were joined in a system implementation project. The three executives were each in a silo within their own organizations, and did not meet or talk with one another. In fact, they each thought the other one was "out to get me" and had different perceptions of what the other person's intentions were. However, these perceptions were incorrect. As it turned out, they were actually on the same page about several pressing project issues. How did I know this? I talked to each one of them individually and asked them what their intentions were. As it turns out, they were in alignment. At the end of my site visit, I had a joint meeting with all three of them and we resolved the issues. No technology required.

Reliance on certifications

IN ADDITION TO the reliance on tools, templates and collaborative software, there has been a movement to requiring project managers to complete the PMP certification. Project Management Professional (PMP) is a credential offered by the Project Management Institute (PMI). As of mid 2009, there were over 350,000 PMP certified individuals worldwide. The credential is obtained by documenting three or five years work experience in project management, completing 35 hours of project management-related training, and scoring a certain percentage of questions on a written, multiple choice examination.[3]

For a large complex project, a PMP certification is just the price of admission as it provides a common language and methodology for project management. However, there are few studies that correlate the success rates of projects to whether or not the project manager is PMP certified. Experience implementing projects of similar scope and nature can be more important than having a PMP as a PMP provides the framework for *managing* large scale projects, not knowledge about specifics regarding system implementations. Organizations that choose 'generic' project managers with PMP certifications, who lack domain knowledge, will surely struggle with elusive project success.

To me, project management experience and domain knowledge about the type software you are implementing is 50% of success. The other 50% lies in understanding the organization and knowing how to navigate the organizational structure to advance project goals. In addition, that second 50% success factor relies heavily on communication skills and business acumen – something not easily obtained through a PMP certification.

Lack of project assurance methodologies

OVER THE LAST several years, there has been an increasing adoption of Independent Verification and Validation (IV&V) for large scale IT projects, especially in the government space. IV&V is defined as follows: "verification and validation is the process conducted by a third party that checks that a product, service, or system meets specifications and that it fulfills its intended purpose. These are critical components of a quality management system such as ISO 9000.

IV&V is comprised of three components:

- Independent ensures the validation is performed by a disinterested or impartial third party.

- Verification is a quality control process that is used to evaluate whether or not a product, service, or system complies with regulations, specifications, or conditions imposed at the start of a development phase. Verification can be in development, scale-up, or production. This is often an internal process.

- Validation is quality assurance process of establishing evidence that provides a high degree of assurance that a product, service, or system accomplishes its intended requirements. This often involves acceptance of fitness for purpose with end users and other product stakeholders." [4]

Just like project management, the IV&V processes have been adopted from other industries such as construction, manufacturing, food and drug and engineering to name a few. The concepts of verification *"Are we building the right thing?"* and validation *"Are we building it right?"* were first introduced in technology for custom software development and the application of quality assurance programs such as ISO and CMMI. These process oriented development projects rely heavily on hands-on software testing to determine if the product built does indeed meet the business requirements. The problem with this approach when implementing packaged software is that the failure points occur long before testing. Sure, IV&V can tactically help reduce software defects to improve user acceptance, but it does not test and validate the strategic direction of the project.

In addition, applying standard IV&V concepts to project management falls short in the following areas:

- No common language or methodology for IV&V software implementation projects. Most projects are glorified project audits that address obvious gaps in deliverables

- Utilize a general project management point of view and miss details associated with packaged software implementation – such as software interdependences and joint organizational responsibilities

- Addresses tactical project issues and does not offer strategic solutions to project issues

The high cost of failure

As MENTIONED IN the previous section, project failure can happen early, causing a ripple effect on your project. In planning your project, you have calculated your project budget, resource / staffing needs and your projected ROI. However, if there is a gap in your requirements that causes delay during the acquisition phase of your project, or worse yet, you leave out key requirements from the strategy phase because of a rushed assessment, the resulting impact will be seen downstream – causing the extension of subsequent project phases. The ripple effect of missing project gaps early during the project will not only create vulnerability and weakness in the project plan integrity, it affects the time line, the overall project cost, realized benefits / ROI calculations and the project team's credibility.

For example, project delay cost can be measured as follows:

Internal and external resources cost – a three month project delay resulting in the extension of two internal resources at $120,000 a year, plus the extension of three consultants at $175 per hour, results in over $350,000 in extra project costs

Delayed operational improvements and realization of operational improvements – a three month project delay with additional resource cost will lower the project return on investment (ROI) by delaying the realization of the system benefits in the form of cost saving and streamlined business processes

Loss of confidence in the project team itself – missed project deadlines result in lower project team morale and organizational skepticism about the viability of the current and future projects

The business case for a better way

HISTORY IS REPEATING itself – the impact of the global recession on technology spending is creating the latest inflection point for enterprise systems. The inflection point will occur when organizations realize that upgrading the application will cost as much as implementing the software in the first place. As the economy improves and beyond, organizations will once again begin enterprise system projects in the form of business process transformation projects, new system implementations or upgrades.

But how can we improve the odds for implementation success? As you can see from our analysis of project failure, projects will continue to fail due to human factors with the most common and fatal failure points occurring early in the project – making the cost of failure exponential.

Inherent in the analysis of failure is the software implementation methodology itself (the waterfall methodology). As a stand-alone, legacy project management methodology, it does not have the checks and balances required to ensure success during the strategy, acquisition and planning stages. It does not provide the mechanisms for project interventions.

By combining the lessons learned with the analysis of why projects fail, the alarming fact is, that after all these years, while the level of expertise in enterprise system implementations has increased, the success rate has not. Future failures are imminent because many organizations lack the ability, tools and knowledge to ensure that projects are delivered on time, on-budget, with user acceptance, or, to put it another way, *organizations lack project assurance.*

The need for project assurance

HOW CAN ANY organization that is considering implementing a large-scale enterprise system disregard the need for project assurance? Project assurance is about making sure that projects are delivered on time, on-budget, with client acceptance. Having project assurance as part of a large-scale system implementation or transformation project helps you:

- control/reduce project costs

- ensure milestones are met

- minimize surprises

- provide objective analysis

- provide peace of mind and trust among executives and project team members

If you don't have a Genie handy, project assurance is the closest thing to an insurance policy for enterprise application software implementations that you can get.

The review meeting: somewhere between a rock and a hard place.

*T*he review meeting was held in the finance department conference room known as 'the rock' because the window had a view of another FirstCorp building's stone façade. In some sort of twisted joke, the conference room down the hall was nicknamed 'the hard place.' Ironically, the project team offices were located between these two conference rooms.

It seems like ages have passed since the executive committee meeting placed the project on hold, Jenny thought to herself, mentally going over the list. Over the last week and a half, we've reviewed all of the project documents, cross-referenced them, interviewed the key participants and developed our findings. Now it's time to present them to the executive committee before the meeting with Cindy. The goal here is not so much to present the findings, because as Bill said, the findings "are what they are" in the sense that they are a factual representation of the situation. The goal is to gain consensus amongst the players and determine the go forward plan.

To give everybody a heads-up, Bill had e-mailed Brett, Mary and Bobby the findings report ahead of time and was able to speak briefly with Brett and Bobby to get their feedback. He was unable to catch up with Mary, who was still knee-deep in HR issues.

"Has everyone had a chance to review the report?" Bill asked. Brett, Mary and Bobby nodded in response. "OK then, let's walk through the assessment. First, as you know, Jenny and I spent a great deal of time reviewing where we are in the project. We reviewed and cross-referenced the critical project documentation from the start of the project and have spoken with each of you. From this assessment, we have gathered our findings, dividing them into the following sections: Project Management, Functional, Technical, and Change Management. Each section has a summary of the current state of the particular area with recommendations for improvements or areas of concern," Bill said.

"Let's start with project management. Overall, the project is showing a red status – meaning that the project team has missed critical milestones and that there are a number of show stopper issues with the software," Bill paused before going on. "On the positive side, we do have a good project management structure to track progress, issues and risks. We just haven't been able to act because the executive committee feels like a decision can't be made without top management – Cindy – being involved."

"Are you sure you want to keep that last part about Cindy?" Mary asked. "I don't think it would be wise to call her out."

"Well, maybe we could change the wording or just bring that up in the course of discussion," said Bill, "but, given the fact that it is such a major issue, don't you think it needs to be addressed?"

"Ummm," Mary started.

"I do," Brett chimed in. "I mean a lot of this is her fault. I think we should call her out."

"I don't think you want to go that far," Bobby interjected.

"We absolutely need to bring this up with Cindy," said Jenny. "If we don't, we won't have the executive support to get what we need. If she wants things to get better, she has two choices: become more involved or delegate more authority."

"Or kill the project," Mary said, cutting her off.

"Or kill the project," Bill agreed, "but that decision is beyond us. Now I don't want to put my head on the chopping block any more than you do, but we need to address this with her. I can leave it off the written report, but bring it up in discussion."

"I would be more comfortable with that approach," Mary submitted.

"OK, then we will go with that," Bill concluded. "If there is nothing else on Project Management, let's move on to the Functional Section."

"On the financial side, the project team is on track with the exception of several critical issues with the software. Jenny is working with Lisa at BusinessWare and the software issues have been escalated to the highest level possible. We are expecting patches and fixes to be delivered no later than next Friday," said Bill.

"I am glad we had that conference call," Jenny chimed in. "Lisa has been super-responsive and I'm seeing progress."

"Good." Everybody agreed.

Bill continued. "As for the HR side, things are not as great. The team is two months behind for various reasons, but mainly because they were late to join the project team and their resources are spread too thin. Mary, do you agree with this assessment?"

"Yes," she replied, "but I would also like to add the discussion that we had with Parnew about converting to their system."

"I think that's a great idea," Bill said. "On the technical side, IT has stabilized the environment. At this point there are no serious issues."

"Well, that is not entirely true," Brett added. "We have to do something about the constant requests for security access, data refreshes and more environments."

"What, you need more business requirements?" Tim said sarcastically.

"No," Brett replied. "I understand that there will be requests and some are legitimate and others are not. I need you and Jenny to do a better job of vetting these requests from the project team and then requesting a reasonable turnaround time for non-critical requests."

"I think we can do that," Jenny said.

"Good, that would make things a hundred times better," said Brett.

"If there is no further discussion of the technical issues, then let's talk Change Management," Bill continued. "As you may have noticed, I did not invite Janice to this meeting because some of this discussion will involve her.

"From what Jenny and I can tell, we are missing the boat on change management and this cutover is going to have a significant impact on the end users. I know from my past company experience that in finance, the users are going to have learn more about both accounting and the new system. No longer are they going to be able to enter smart codes for transactions that are going to create the accounting entries themselves, they are going to have to learn and enter the accounting entries themselves."

"From talking with the HR VP at Parnew, the situation will be similar for HR staff," Mary added. "I have to say I am very concerned about this."

"This is one area we need help, but I am not sure we have the people in-house to do it," Jenny said, and added, "Bill and I were thinking we could get a proposal from Bobby on what it would cost for CYA to take this over."

"I think we can do that," Bobby quickly replied. He always seemed to be more alert when new services were involved.

"OK," Bill asked, "does everybody agree with these findings?"

A unified "Yes."

"Great," Bill paused, "but before we move to on the recommendations, let's summarize the findings:

1. The project status is red and there are a number of show stopper issues with the software.

2. With a few exceptions, the financials implementation is on track, but HR is behind and slipping.

3. The technical environment is stable, but better processes need to be put in place regarding requests from the project team.

4. The change management and training effort will be significant and we do not have the resources in-house to meet the project scope and time line."

"So here are my thoughts on recommendations," Bill said, approaching the white board.

1. We need executive involvement, either in the form of Cindy or empowering the executive team to make the go-forward decisions.

"I agree," Mary said, "just tread lightly with that one."
"Will do," Bill continued.

2. We need to escalate the critical issues with BusinessWare. We have already started this with our conference call the other day and, as Jenny mentioned, the vendor has been very responsive.

"And, although this one is not as critical as the other," Bill stated, "let's just get it out of the way:

3. Implement a vetting and prioritized vetting process for project team requests to IT.

"Now for some tougher issues. What do you guys think we should do in the functional areas?" Bill asked.

"Well, it sounds like, for the most part, the financial project is on track," said Bobby.

"Agreed," Jenny replied.

"You know what I would like to see?" asked Mary. "At this point, we really should put HR on hold to conduct an assessment of the new company's HR system and determine if it is a viable solution. We completed a lot of remediation work towards Y2K, so I think we have a better chance of making our old system Y2K compliant versus making the date to implement the new system."

"Plus, if we continue down the current path, we may not have the resources or ability to digest both a new HR and financial system at this time," Brett added.

"That's a good point," said Mary.

"Well, what about our consultants?" Tim asked.

"We would roll them off," Bill replied.

"You know," Bobby started, "you could use the cost savings on not continuing with HR for change management and training."

"Good idea, Bobby, but given all the money we are spending with you guys, we are expecting the go-live party to be at your lake house," Jenny said.

"I think we can do that," Bobby replied with a grin.

"OK, so that takes care of HR and financials," said Bill. "But what should we do with Janice?"

"I have a thought," Brett added. "Janice was the project manager for our current HR system, she would be a good person to lead the assessment of the HR system conversion to Parnew's system. Mary, would you be comfortable with that?"

"Very comfortable," Mary replied.

"Good, then it's a win-win solution," Bill said. "So, in summary, our final recommendations are as follows:

4. Continue with the financials implementation and critical issues resolution.

5. Place the HR system on hold and conduct an assessment to determine if we should convert to the new company's systems.

6. Use the cost savings to have CYA Partners provide change management services.

"Are each of you comfortable with the recommendations?" Bill asked.

Everybody nodded in agreement.

"Good, I will put together some slides for the meeting with Cindy and will send them to you before the meeting," said Bill. "Also, I appreciate your open-mindedness for this assessment as I knew many of you were skeptical to begin with. I know that these recommendations are high level and there is a lot of work for us to do, but I think they are reflective of the best path forward. You all have done a lot of good work and we are too close on finance to stop now. Freeing up some resources from the HR side to apply to change management will definitely help get us across the finish line. See you Friday."

The meeting with Cindy

As Jenny walked into the restaurant, Bill was in the lobby waiting for her.

"Hi Jenny, good to see you." Bill shook her hand warmly. "How have you been?"

"Can't complain," she responded. "How about you? You look good ... like you've lost some weight."

"Hey, I took a cue from you. I started running and eating healthy. No more coffee and donuts for breakfast," Bill grinned.

"That's great," Jenny said. "I think our table is ready."

As they walked to the table, she couldn't help but think back to that fateful Friday meeting in Cindy's office.

Cindy's office was located on the 20th floor executive suite of the FirstCorp headquarters. The executive suite had great panoramic views of the city and was decorated with the awards, marketing slogans and framed articles about the company's successes, not the failures or train wrecks.

Jenny had felt immediately that their fate would be determined in next hour. Everybody was a little nervous, even Bobby and Charles. Both of them had plenty of executive interaction, but they knew the situation was serious and that there was always the potential to lose business or profits. Even though they were senior executives with their firms, they, too, reported to people who demanded results.

They were led to a waiting area and told that Cindy was wrapping up a conference call with Ted about the Parnew acquisition. They waited nervously in the waiting room, fidgeting and making small talk. After a half hour, Cindy emerged and asked them to get set-up to present while she stopped by her office to grab a bottle of water.

Cindy Jackson was the COO of FirstCorp, a job she had earned working her way up through the ranks. She started out as an administrative assistant and quickly rose through management, tackling everyone and anything in her way. She had gained a reputation as a tough-nosed negotiator who made quick decisions. Everyone knew that if you were going to present to Cindy, you had to have your ducks in row. The same held true for our project. It was initially spearheaded by Cindy, but after the Parnew acquisition, she was needed elsewhere. The problem was that she never really gave up the position of executive sponsor of the project that was now in jeopardy.

Cindy walked in with her portfolio and bottle of water. Despite the fact that it was 4:00 p.m. on a Friday afternoon, she appeared as crisp as ever and seemed in no hurry to go anywhere other than on to more meetings.

Great, Jenny thought. Hope no one has plans for dinner.

"So have you had a chance to settle in here at FirstCorp yet, Bill?" Cindy asked, cracking a smile.

"Oh yeah, out of the frying pan and into the fire," Bill shot back.

"I guess you didn't expect this trial by fire on your first two weeks of the job," Cindy said.

"No, not exactly how I imagined things, but it is what it is," Bill said as he handed out the presentation. "Let's get started, shall we?"

The final report was not more than a few pages long, but in order to get the major points across to Cindy, Bill and Jenny had condensed the report to a couple of slides.

Bill opened the meeting. "First off, Cindy, thanks for giving us some of your time today. At your request, the team here, led by Jenny and me, has conducted an assessment of the current state of the project. As you know, the status of the project is not good. From our assessment, which consisted of a thorough review of all project documentation and interviews with all the key players, if the project was allowed to continue to progress in its current form, it would most likely fail. If you look at the first slide, you will see an outline of our process, the documentation we reviewed and the people we interviewed."

"OK, sounds like a good process, Bill, so what are the results?" asked Cindy.

"Well, let's start with the good news," stated Bill. "The financial implementation is on track, and, while we've had a few critical issues with the BusinessWare applications, Charles and his team have escalated the issues with their development people. We expect fixes to be delivered by next week."

"Well, that is good news, Charles," said Cindy. "We've spent a great deal of money with you and we expect that this project will mean as much to BusinessWare as it does to FirstCorp."

"It absolutely does, Cindy," responded Charles. "We've had a few miscommunications, but I can assure you that things are back on track. I'm getting daily updates from our team on the status of your issues. You have our full commitment."

"Good, we expect nothing less," Cindy responded. "OK, Bill, that's the good news – now what's the bad?"

"The HR implementation is behind for a number of reasons," Bill continued.

1. HR was late to the project and did not have time to fully define their requirements.

2. The project is taking place in the middle of open enrollment and the resources are spread too thin with the Parnew merger.

"Well, this is disappointing news, but I understand the situation. We just can't stop the HR implementation," Cindy responded. "Can it be fixed?"

"We aren't sure yet," Bill said. "Through our assessment, Mary brought up the idea of converting to Parnew's system or finishing the remediation of the legacy system. Either way, given the resource requirements, we are not sure we can complete both the financial and HR implementations."

"Bobby, what is your take on this?" Cindy asked. "I believe it was your firm who recommended that we do both. If we cancelled HR, we would expect some concessions from you."

"Well, we didn't anticipate the merger and we underestimated the impact of open enrollment on HR," replied Bobby. "I don't want to pre-empt Bill, but that will come later in the report."

"Good, so what is the team's recommendation?" asked Cindy.

"We need to stop the HR implementation and look at either moving onto Parnew's system or finishing the remediation and implement the BusinessWare modules later. Either way, we need more time to study the options," declared Bill.

"What about the integration between timekeeping and project costing?" asked Cindy, "Wasn't that why we were doing this in the first place?"

Boy, she has a good memory, Jenny thought to herself. *I guess you don't get to Cindy's level unless you are pretty sharp.*

"We think we can handle that through an interface," Tim offered.

"Holy cow, where was that idea seven months ago before we headed down this path?" Cindy erupted. The room fell silent.

"Let's go ahead with the assessment findings and not worry about how we got here," Bill said quietly, breaking the tension. "We can table that discussion for the contract review with CYA."

"OK, so finance is on track, HR is off track. What else?" Cindy asked.

"Two things," said Bill. "First, in order for finance to be successful, we need more of a focus on change management. We have asked Bobby to develop a scope of work proposal to provide that service. We can divert some of the funds from the HR implementation and training to change management – and given the situation with the HR project, I am sure Bobby will give us a good deal on the services."

"Alright, what is the second thing?" Cindy asked.

"Well, we know that you are tied up with the Parnew acquisition, but we need to make sure we have more of your time for decision making or that you empower the executive team to make decisions. Some of these unresolved issues have been floating around for a while because there is confusion about who can make decisions," Bill explained quietly.

"I assumed that you guys were making most of the decisions, but items of this magnitude need to be brought to my attention. Given my schedule, I'm unable to make the current executive committee meetings, but I need to be kept abreast of what is going on," Cindy stated. "From here on, let's set a 15 minute, bi-weekly briefing, in person or conference call, with all of us – Bill, Brett, Mary, Bobby, Charles and Jenny – preferably before the day gets started, to make sure you have my attention or if there are decisions that I need to be involved in."

"Sounds good," Bill replied.

"Do you think we can make the go-live date for financials?" Cindy asked.

"Probably," Bill replied. "We may need to do some more analysis to be sure."

"We cannot keep changing the date," Cindy stated flatly. "If we need to change it again, we better make sure that this is the last time we do it."

"Got it," everybody replied.

"Bobby, when can you get us that proposal?" Cindy inquired pointedly.

"I should have it early next week," Bobby responded.

"Let's do this," Bill summarized. "We have a couple action items: one, we need do some more research on the go-live date for financials; two, get a time line for the HR assessment; and three, get a proposal from Bobby for additional change management services. In addition, we'll go back and do our due diligence in these areas and then we will regroup with you at the same time next Friday. Are you comfortable with that, Cindy?"

"Yes," she nodded her head, punching the meeting date and time into her smartphone.

"Is everyone else comfortable with this approach?" asked Bill.

"I'm not sure that is enough time ... " Mary and Tim both protested, but stopped once they got a glare from Cindy.

"Ah, sure, I think we can get it done," Bobby broke in.

"One more thing," Cindy said, "I appreciate the work you guys did on this assessment and I am glad we stepped back for a minute to look at the situation. But make no mistake; I'm not happy with all that has happened surrounding the project, so let's keep our eyes on the ball moving forward. Understood?"

Everyone nodded just as if they had just been scolded by the teacher.

"Alright then, I will see you next week," Cindy said. "I need to give Ted an update. Bobby, you may want to take your family out to dinner and a movie tonight, otherwise Ted may be paying you one of those evening visits."

"Got it, thanks for the heads up," Bobby said, his eyes wide open as he headed for the door.

SECTION 2:

PROJECT ASSURANCE THROUGH COLLABORATIVE INTERVENTION

Bill and Jenny catch up

The Oak Room served marvelous seafood and was always crowded at lunch. Bill met Jenny at 11:30 a.m. Bill was an early riser and usually ready for lunch around 11:00 a.m., but could stretch it since nobody else was ready to eat lunch that early. The waitress greeted them and led them to a table by the window – another perk of beating the lunch hour crowd.

I bet he orders the Caesar salad with salmon, Jenny thought to herself. Jenny had been to lunch with Bill on dozens of occasions, and nine times out of ten, he ordered a Caesar salad with salmon.

They sat down and Bill pushed his menu aside as there was no need to open it.

Yep, Caesar salad it is. Jenny thought as she smiled.

"So, how is the family?" Bill asked, smiling in return.

"Great – Jamie is eleven and Monica just had her fifth birthday party last Saturday," Jenny grinned. "It was a princess theme and I'm still exhausted."

"Wow ... time flies," observed Bill.

"Tell me about it," Jenny responded. "It seems like we spend all our time running around between dance and soccer."

"Been there," Bill replied. "And how is your consulting business going?"

"Going well enough, but it's been a bit slow lately with the economy and everything," Jenny remarked. "There's not a lot of new project spending, but I've had some steady work from my past clients and every once in a while I get a call from CYA Partners to do some sub-contracting. How about you? What's new at FirstCorp?"

"Things are still crazy," Bill chuckled. "Ted is still on an acquisition binge, so it's constant integration with the new companies. In fact, this latest acquisition with DataTech has been a killer because they're about 60% of our size, so you can imagine the issues."

"And how is Cindy?" Jenny asked.

"Cindy retired about six months ago," Bill said. "I took over her role as COO."

"Wow, congratulations, Bill," Jenny exclaimed, and then quickly added, "I think."

"Yeah thanks, it's definitely a challenging role," Bill grinned. "Plus, it's always a pleasure dealing with Ted."

The waitress came to take their lunch selections. Jenny ordered the turkey and Swiss Panini while Bill –you guessed it – ordered the Caesar salad with salmon.

"So, any new projects on the horizon?" Jenny asked curiously.

"Actually, yes. That's why I wanted to meet with you today," Bill said.

Jenny leaned forward in anticipation.

"As you know, we've been on the BusinessWare platform for some time," Bill looked out the window at the crepe myrtle tree in full purple bloom. "Gosh, I guess it'll be eleven years in November."

"I know, can you believe it?" asked Jenny. "I was thinking about the original implementation project on the drive over to meet you."

"Well, we certainly got our act together after that project," Bill remembered. "And, although we had some bumps in the road along the way, our upgrades and projects to add new functionality and additional modules were much smoother. But now things are a bit different."

"What do you mean?" Jenny asked.

"I'll get right to the point," Bill responded. "We need to realize some cost savings. Despite our acquisition binge, we have not been immune to the economy. We are facing two major beach heads – FirstCorp's systems and DataTech's. We are both on the same BusinessWare human resources system, and for finance, they use FSI. Interestingly enough, although FirstCorp has double the revenues of DataTech, they have twice the number of employees that we do, given their business. Also, they have implemented a shared services model, something we have only recently talked about, and all of their IT systems have been outsourced to BigSI."

"Interesting," Jenny said, as she began to run through the possibilities in her head. *Maybe he wants me to be the financials project manager. This is perfect. I will be at FirstCorp forever. Maybe I can start that kitchen remodeling project my husband and I were thinking about.*

"So are you both on the same version of BusinessWare HR?" she queried Bill.

"No, we are on 6.4 and they are on 7.5," he said.

"Wasn't Version 8 just released?" she asked.

"Yep, but given the economy and all the merger activity, we have not been able to stay current. Plus we are still on Version 6.4 for finance and DataTech uses FSI – which I don't know much about," Bill explained.

"You know, I do have some experience with FSI, but it's been a while," Jenny said, as their meal arrived.

"Let's eat. I am positively starving," Bill said, as Jenny's thoughts drifted to the project possibilities. She began to wonder if she'd have enough time to stop at the Kitchen Expo on the way to pick up the kids from school and look at designer kitchen cabinets.

The project

While Jenny and Bill enjoyed lunch, the conversation bounced back and forth between business and personal topics. A lot of the catching up had to do with people that they had worked with and what they were doing now. From the original implementation team: Cindy had retired; Brett is now CIO of FirstCorp, but still as bitter as ever; and Mary is now in charge of corporate communications and investor relations. Interestingly, Tim, who was Jenny's original counterpart with CYA Partners, had taken a full time job with FirstCorp and is now in charge of the Project Management Office (PMO) reporting to Brett. Bobby, a partner with CYA, was still managing the account, but permanently moved to his lake house when his kids went off to college.

"So, tell me a little bit more about the project ... " Jenny asked Bill, eager to get back to the opportunity at hand and her new kitchen.

"It's complicated, there are a lot of variables involved. We are behind on application versions; we have multiple applications between the companies; we need to streamline processes and cut costs. To accomplish all this, we need to consider some new business models such as shared services and possibly outsourcing – taking a cue from DataTech," Bill responded and paused. "Given the magnitude and complexities, we decided to take a step back and really look at the big picture. So a couple of months ago, we hired Bobby's firm to come in and do a study."

"Let me guess," Jenny chortled. "Their recommendation was 'transformation'."

"Of course, we knew that going in," Bill chuckled back. "But seriously, a lot of what they said makes sense and will help us make some quantum leaps forward. But I'm not convinced we have the time or money to implement everything they recommended. So we are going to start with HR."

"Are you going to convert them to FirstCorp's BusinessWare platform?" Jenny queried.

"Yes, but we are going to have to upgrade first or as part of the conversion project," Bill replied. "And that is still up in the air. We are going to outsource the IT portion of our systems to BigSI."

"That's news. What does Brett think about that?" Jenny stared at Bill.

"As you could probably guess, he isn't thrilled," Bill said, "but he knows it makes sense."

"And what about financials?" she inquired.

"That is definitely phase two," Bill said, as Jenny's dreams of the new kitchen vanished.

"So how can I help, Bill?" Jenny asked.

"I'm not sure I have a defined role for you, Jenny," he said, "but I wanted to have a conversation with you because you definitely bring a lot of value in terms of your knowledge of big system implementations and the issues facing our organization."

"Well, I can be the project manager for you, if that is what you are asking," she replied.

"I think that would be a great idea, but ..." Bill started, but Jenny interrupted him. "Let me guess – I don't have the experience with the HR apps?"

"No that isn't it, Jenny," Bill said quickly. "We have plenty of people, most of whom could do the job. But we don't have the budget to bring you in. We're already running lean with the economy and still letting people go as pat of the merger consolidation. More cuts will eventually come as we move to shared services and outsourcing. So politically and financially, it doesn't make sense to bring you in as a full time project manager. But, given what you could bring to the table, I wanted to discuss if we could find some creative ways that you could be involved in the project."

"It sounds like you have a team in place, Bill," Jenny mused. "And with BigSI on the line for delivery, what are you concerned about?"

"Frankly, I'm concerned about a couple of things," Bill reacted. "And the first concern is gaps."

"Gaps?" she asked.

"Yes, gaps," Bill replied. "We have a lot of players involved in this implementation: two HR teams (FirstCorp and DataTech); two IT departments; the Project Management Office and BigSI. As we put this project together, given all the players, I'm concerned that there will be gaps in expectations, scope, timeframe, budget, requirements and the contract. And based on the size of this effort, if we don't get this project off on the right foot, it will be tough to get back on track."

"Oh, I'm sure that there will be gaps, Bill," Jenny said. "But what else are you concerned about?"

"Objectivity," Bill stated. "Jenny, I need somebody to provide an objective point of view. Not only for the other players involved, but if FirstCorp is not doing their part, I need someone to get in our faces and tell us. Now that I'm COO, I'm not sure that I am getting honest feedback from my team. And of course, all the other players have their own agenda ..."

"So are you looking for me to provide independent verification and validation?" asked Jenny.

"Not exactly, but something similar and better," Bill said mysteriously. "First off, let's not use that description 'IV&V' or the PMO will want to get involved and I need someone to make sure that they are *doing their job as well. Secondly, I need something beyond IV&V. I need someone to look not only at the current state of the project, but beyond the indicators to see what is coming down the tracks. And if there is a problem, I need someone to help us define and implement a solution."*

"That sounds like a great idea, Bill," Jenny said, "but to be realistic, you just said that you don't have any budget."

"I said that I don't have the budget to bring you in full time, but I do have some money," Bill amended his earlier words. "To me, this is like an insurance policy for the implementation. We simply cannot afford not to have it." Bill paused. "Are you interested?"

"Yes, do you have time for coffee or dessert?" Jenny asked. "We can continue this discussion."

Bill checked his watch. "I have about another 15 minutes, so let's order and continue."

Jenny flagged down the waitress.

More than just dessert

" **S** *o, exactly what do you have in mind?" Jenny asked, knowing Bill usually has the answers to his own questions.*

"Well," Bill grinned, "I was thinking that you would come in on a routine basis and conduct an assessment of where the project is at each major milestone. As I said before, I am concerned about the gaps that currently exist or will develop based on all the parties involved. I'm sure we could identify and prevent the gaps before they occur."

"I understand," Jenny said. "It's similar to the project intervention that we conducted on the original BusinessWare implementation. Talk about a project that had requirements gaps – they could have passed for the Grand Canyon."

Bill chuckled. "Exactly, you could even follow the same approach. At critical points in the project lifecycle, you could review our project documents, cross-reference them, and then interview the key players to make sure that all the documents and project participants are on the same page. Based on this research, you could provide us a report of your findings."

"That sounds fairly straightforward," Jenny responded. "I think I can handle that."

"Good. I need you to put together a proposal for me that will outline the project costs based on each assessment and how many of the assessments you think we will need," Bill wasted no time.

"Well, I guess that depends on the size of the project," Jenny said, thinking out loud.

"Use your best guess, Jenny," Bill offered. "You know our organization well enough and the challenges you'll face, so I trust your judgment. If you have any questions, just shoot me an e-mail."

"OK," Jenny responded, "will do."

"Look I need to run, I just got a text from Ted and his pants are on fire," Bill placed his cloth napkin on the table and stood. "Can you handle the check? I'll get it next time."

"Sure, Bill," she replied. "I'll chalk this up as a sales lunch. I'll be in touch."

"Seriously, Jenny," Bill said, "When do you think you can get me the proposal? The project is already somewhat underway."

"No later than noon on Thursday," calculated Jenny. "That gives me two full days to put it together."

"Great, I'm looking forward to seeing it," Bill began to leave. "Give my best to your family."

"Will do," Jenny called as he began to walk away. "I'll contact you on Thursday."

After Bill left, Jenny gazed at the flowering tree outside the window and finished her coffee. She thought about the project while she settled the check. This project should be fairly straightforward. She would just be repeating the same steps several times throughout the project. Plus, Bill would be there to back her up so she knew her findings and *recommendations would be heard. And even better, if she ran into any issues or roadblocks he would be able to clear them for her.*

Since the waitress was taking her time, she decided to type some notes into her smartphone about the project and her conversation with Bill.

Large transformation project.

BusinessWare upgrade.

Convert DataTech.

Transition to BigSI.

Conduct point in time assessment consisting of document review, cross-reference and interviews.

Develop report. Present findings and recommendations to Bill. Determine when to conduct assessment.

Proposal due Thursday at noon.

Wait on the kitchen renovation.

What is collaborative intervention?

HOW DO YOU know if failure lies ahead? Often you don't. But if you stand back and look at the situation as if you were watching a movie, you may see the signs of impending disaster. Picture this scene: a train speeding down the track; a hurried driver in a car trying to make it across the tracks as the train rounds the curve; the conductor not paying attention; the crossing bars going down; the red lights flashing; the bells ringing. Watching the movie, how can you miss what is about to happen?

Picturing the project as a movie works if you can stand back from the project, but, the truth is that most people on the project team can't see the train wreck that is about to occur, or if they do see it, they don't know how to stop it. That is why collaborative intervention is so innovative: it is a process to avert disaster by identifying the warning signs and taking preventative action.

Collaborative intervention is a project assurance methodology designed to align project expectations, resources and scope with the goal of increasing the project's probability of success. Collaborative intervention is different from other project assurance methodologies in that it addresses key project failure points before they occur. How? By creating a collaborative environment composed of key project stakeholders to identify and resolve project issues and avert roadblocks as they arise.

Most project teams may not encounter one large disaster, but a series of small disasters that can lead up to larger failure. Like the train wreck scenario above, different parts of the project team may be unaware that they are on a collision course. Individual events, such as the driver running late or the conductor being distracted, may be caused by events that took place earlier. The same is true for project failure. For example, not conducting a needs assessment; missing requirements; choosing the wrong software or implementation partner; or underestimating the impact of change can all be identified early on and corrected to lessen the downstream impact.

Collaborative intervention is an ongoing process that evaluates warning signs at the points at which they are likely to begin to occur in the project. Collaborative intervention allows project managers and executives to take action, to monitor the situation to make sure that the issues are resolved, and if not, adjust accordingly. By establishing a framework of collaborative intervention, organizations can ensure that project failure points are averted before they occur and the disastrous train wreck never materializes.

What collaborative intervention means to you

SIMILAR IN CONCEPT to Independent Verification and Validation (IV&V), collaborative intervention is the project assurance methodology that lets you verify that project requirements are met and validate that the project implementation will meet the requirements. However, collaborative intervention differs from a traditional IV&V project in the following critical ways:

1. **It's comprehensive.** Project management IV&V focuses on tactical projects issues such as hands-on testing of software to make sure that the product built matches detailed requirements, where as collaborative intervention takes a more comprehensive approach to not only have checkpoints to ensure tactical deployment, but also checkpoints for strategic issues such as project alignment with organizational goals and strategy.

2. **It's a smarter start.** Project management IV&V methodologies often start in the project planning phase after a strategy has been defined and software has been purchased. Collaborative intervention defines the beginning of the project as the initial strategy phase when project goals, objectives, budgets and plans are formulated, and subsequently, software and services are purchased. Since many project failure points are conceived in the early stages of the project, it makes sense to put the collaborative intervention framework in place at the beginning of the project to ensure success from the start.

3. **It's friendly.** Project management IV&V methodologies focus on the science of software implementation – what is quantifiable and tangible. Collaborative intervention, unlike IV&V, provides an ongoing structure for realistic issue resolution based on intangible human factors – trust, common goals and communication.

4. **It's proactive.** The collaborative intervention process is proactive, whereas IV&V is reactive. Collaborative intervention not only reviews the current status of the project, but also ensures that scope, resources and funding are appropriately aligned for upcoming project phases and activities.

5. **It's preventative.** Collaborative intervention creates a structure of change and involvement for project sponsors, executives and project managers. Collaboration with an outside expert adds both value to the project implementation and protection against the high cost of failure. The interventionist delivers not only know-how, but also assists in navigating the organization by creating a collaborative team of decision makers that can remove project roadblocks.

The Collaborative intervention process

 OLLABORATIVE INTERVENTION IS comprised of three steps: identify, assess, and intervene.

Collaborative Intervention

1. **Identify** – The first step of the collaborative intervention process is to identify where the project is in the implementation lifecycle, so that you understand **when** to intervene. Once determined, you can know what to look for and what the likely issues may be.

2. **Assess** – The second step of the collaborative intervention process is to assess. The assessment is a top-to-bottom evaluation of **what** to look for during the project to help you align project expectations, resources and scope with the goal of increasing the project's probability of success.

3. **Intervene** – The final stage of the collaborative intervention process is to intervene. The collaborative intervention process outlines **how** to intervene by presenting the findings of the assessment and working with the project team to develop an implementation plan to address the findings.

At the end of the day, collaborative intervention gives you the *when, what and how* answers you need to assure project success. It helps you to identify and resolve the strategic, tactical and intangible issues before they become insurmountable. Collaborative intervention gives you the tools and techniques you need to investigate and defuse volatile situations within the organization and the project team.

And best of all, collaborative intervention gives you (and everyone else involved) peace of mind that the project is on the right track.

How to become an interventionist
Identify

YOUR FIRST STEP in the collaborative intervention process is to identify where the project is in the implementation lifecycle to know when to intervene. That knowledge will help you to understand what to look for and what the likely issues may be at that particular stage of the implementation.

Collaborative Intervention

As you know, collaborative intervention addresses project failure points before they occur. If we take the top reasons projects fail and overlay them across the project implementation lifecycle, what you'll see is that while the reasons for project failure are present throughout the implementation, all of them have potentially occurred at least once by the third stage of the project: planning.

If you fail to address these potential failure issues early on, they will linger and grow malignantly throughout the project, causing further issues downstream. Historically based upon when failure is likely to occur within the traditional stages of the project lifecycle, I have identified six key points in time where an assessment and intervention will have the greatest impact.

Reasons Project Fail	Strategy	Acquisition	Planning	Design	Development	Testing	Roll-out
1. Lack of Top Mgt. Commitment	X	X	X	X	X	X	X
2. Unrealistic Expectations	X	X	X	X	X	X	
3. Poor Requirements Definition	X	X		X			
4. Improper Package Selection		X					
5. Gaps between software and requirements		X		X			
6. Inadequate Resources			X	X	X	X	
7. Underestimating Time and Costs			X	X	X		
8. Poor Project Management			X	X	X	X	
9. Underestimating Impact of Change			X		X		X
10. Lack of Training / Education			X		X	X	X

I often refer to conducting the intervention at these critical stages in the system implementation lifecycle as 'sampling the soup.' Just as a master chef samples the soup and adjusts the flavors throughout the cooking process, a project executive can intervene at these critical stages in a project's lifecycle to ensure that the project is compliant with best practices, project gaps are being addressed, and expectations are being properly managed.

The six critical stages to intervene in a project are as follows:

1. During strategy phase, before the business case is presented for approval and funding. The purpose of the first intervention is to

address top management's commitment to the project, expectations and requirements definition.

2. During the acquisition phase, towards the end of the vendor selection process, before vendors are finalized and negotiations begin. The purpose of the second intervention is to address the software and services selection and gaps between the proposed software and/or services and the business requirements.

3. Towards the end of the planning phase after the initial drafts of the Project Charter, Detailed Project Plan and Change Management Plans have been developed. The purpose of the third intervention is to ensure that there is a strong project management methodology in place, that the project has adequate resources and that the time line and scope are realistic.

4. Towards the end of the design phase after the initial drafts of the System Design Documentation have been developed. The purpose of the fourth intervention is to ensure that there are minimal gaps between the software and the business requirements, the organization understands the impact of the change and the project has adequate resources allocated.

5. The fifth intervention should be conducted towards the end of the development phase. The purpose is to ensure that the project management methodology for testing is in place, the impact of organizational change is being addressed and the proposed education and training plans will meet user requirements.

6. The final intervention should be conducted towards the end of the testing and training phase. The purpose of the sixth intervention is to ensure that top management is committed to the project for the system cut over and the next phases of

the project, that there are adequate resources in place for the go-live, and that the education and training provided has sufficiently prepared the users for using the new system.

Ideally, the collaborative intervention structure is in place from the beginning of the project. These six critical stages serve as a guide as to when to conduct project assessments and what to look for. Collaborative intervention provides project assurance throughout the implementation. However, if the structure is not in place, then these critical stages will also serve as a guide for conducting an intervention at any point in time during the project as well as a guide to knowing when to conduct future interventions for project assurance.

Assess

YOUR NEXT STEP in the collaborative intervention process is to know what to assess. There are many elements to consider in this assessment. Having a strategy to investigate and determine what the issues are is critical before you can effectively deal with them.

Collaborative Intervention

The assessment stage focuses on what is required to identify the warning signs or trouble indicators.

You begin by asking questions such as these — and listening to the answers:

- Are the conditions right for a train wreck?

- Are we looking forward to see if danger lies ahead or are we heads-down managing status to the next set of project deliverables?

- Everything is on track – the lights are green. What is there to worry about?

Often, with a large-scale project team, everyone is focused on their particular task or relying on what is on paper while not looking deeper. Your role is to investigate further. Ask how the project team feels. Do they sense imminent danger? Is there a general air of disillusionment? Do they have a sinking feeling in their gut?

At this stage in critical intervention, your assessment focuses on digging into project issues, cross- referencing documentation, and interviewing stakeholders to identify warning signs in terms of expectations, time frames and work streams. As I mentioned in the previous section, for a full collaborative intervention, assessment occurs during the six intervention points. The process for each is the same and is based on the following best practices:

1. **Identify the real issues.** At the leadership level, you need to develop an executive dialog that allows business and organizational issues to be identified and analyzed with clarity and without emotion. Continue this dialog throughout the implementation process. Remove organizational barriers both within the organization and with third party vendors. All parties should be aligned with the common goal of project success.

2. **Set realistic time frames.** Don't rely on the existing schedule. Many organizations will set overly optimistic go-live dates in spite of the realities and limitations of the actual project. For example, the design phase extends ... but the time line doesn't. You must monitor project progress throughout the

implementation and start discussions regarding key project dates early in the project's lifecycle to avoid downstream impacts.

3. **Align the work streams.** You need to identify, align and continuously monitor work streams to ensure smooth progress throughout the organization. Understand dependencies between work streams during project plan development to ensure proper resource allocations and project time frames. Continue to monitor the interdependencies throughout the project.

4. **Look beyond the indicators.** Contrary to popular opinion, green may actually be red. Realistic monitoring and analysis of progress of the implementation can show that even though all project management indicators are green, warning signs indicate endangered components. If indicators are only addressing past phases, but not addressing readiness for upcoming project tasks and activities, they are definitely trailing indicators and not trustworthy predictions of the future.

5. **Manage the expectations.** Critical to maintaining control of the project, you need to manage the confluence of overly optimistic go-live dates against outside influences and interdependencies, such as available resources and realistic expectations. Set realistic expectations upfront and keep expectations current in the mind of project team members so that they don't lose sight of the forest while maneuvering around a tree.

6. **Seek objectivity.** Assessments conducted by an outside expert add both value to the project implementation and protection against the high cost of failure. Expertise delivers the know-how and the objective oversight needed to overcome organizational roadblocks. It also provides you with peace of mind. Assess-

ments should be conducted by an executive project manager or software implementation expert who has managed enough projects successfully to know how to recognize subtle indicators, intervene to accommodate the situation, and adjust expectations accordingly.

Each collaborative intervention assessment is composed of seven steps:

1. The expectations meeting
2. Review project documentation
3. Cross-reference documentation
4. Interview key participants
5. Determine areas of concern/recommendations
6. Review findings with key participants
7. Final report/areas for follow-up

1. **The expectations meeting.** Each assessment begins with an expectations meeting. This is a meeting conducted with all the key project participants. At this meeting, the expectations for the assessment are discussed and agreed upon with all parties present. In addition, you should discuss the time line for the assessment of documents that are to be reviewed, the people that are to be interviewed, and the assessment review process itself. Obtain agreement on all of these points and you will have set the independent tone for the assessment.

2. **Review project documentation**. After the expectations meeting has been conducted, your next step is to collect the relevant project documentation for this particular phase of the assessment. Based on the phase of the project, this documentation may vary. For example, during the project planning phase, the documentation may consist of the statement of work, the project charter, the resource allocation plan, the detailed project

plan and the potential change management plan. Your purpose in reviewing the documentation is to gain an understanding of the project direction and the documentation that has been in place to guide the project, as well as to gain an understanding of project direction without having to conduct in-depth interviews about the project with each team member.

3. **Cross-reference documentation**. After the project documentation has been reviewed, the next step in the point in time assessment is to cross-reference the documentation. The interventionist should cross-reference documentation to ensure that there is consistency among project deliverables and to identify the gaps that may occur in expectations, costs, resources and budget, as well as to identify potential solutions. For example, during the procurement process many parties may be involved with writing the statement of work or the statement of work may have varied from the original request for proposal. This happens frequently because the statements of work are often transitioned from the procurement and/or sales team to the legal team to the delivery team. Because of these handoffs, it is always a good idea to go back and cross-reference documents to make sure that you're buying what you intended to buy as scope and delivery assumptions are often changed and added during negotiations.

4. **Interview key participants.** After conducting a thorough review and cross-referencing of project deliverables and documents, it is a good idea to interview the people who wrote documents, approved and signed off on the documents. By interviewing key participants, the interventionist can determine if the project vision has been successfully translated into project execution. In addition, interviewing key participants helps the

interventionist identify potential budget roadblocks, political concerns or other constraints that would not be apparent by just reading the project deliverables. Information gained in these interviews is critical to understanding the complexities of the relationships among the parties involved in the project as well as to understand what has and has not been successful in past projects within the organization. Interviews are also a great tool you can use to uncover people's fears and concerns and gain an understanding of what the organization is trying to accomplish. Without conducting interviews, the interventionist is left without a mechanism to build relationships with key project stakeholders that will allow for downstream issue resolution.

5. **Determine areas of concern and recommendations**. After all documentation has been reviewed and cross-referenced and all key participants interviewed, the interventionist now has the information needed to develop the areas of concern for this point of time assessment. Based on the project phase, the number of issues and areas of concerns will vary, however, the issues identified will represent gaps in terms of requirements, expectations, cost, budget, or resources. It is the responsibility of the interventionist to not only identify these issues and areas of concern, but also provide recommended solutions. As I mentioned before, collaborative intervention is a proactive methodology where ideas and solutions are developed to solve problems, rather than merely identified as in a normal project audit.

6. **Review findings with key participants.** After the interventionist has developed a list of concerns or recommendations, it is time to review the findings with the key project participants. This process is actually done twice. First, the findings

are reviewed during informal discussions held individually with the key participants to ensure that nothing has been misinterpreted in the point time assessment and to make sure that the key participants are briefed on the findings prior to a meeting of all stakeholders. By having an informal discussion with the key participants prior to the formal meeting, the interventionist can gauge the team member's reaction to the findings as well as preliminarily discuss solutions. This also provides the key participants with time to research findings that they may not have been aware of or brainstorm solutions prior to the formal meeting. The second time the findings are reviewed with key participants, everyone should be informed and aware of all of the issues and be prepared to discuss solutions. By being prepared in the first discussion, the participants have already bought into the recommendations and solutions. If they disagree, the interventionist can be prepared to defend the concerns and recommendations.

7. **Final report/areas for follow-up.** As a final step in the process, the interventionist documents the point in time assessment by summarizing the process for the point in time assessment and the findings and recommendations into a final report. This document marks the completion of the point in time assessment for this project phase. However, the final report serves as the input for the next point in time assessment. This is important because leftover action items or unresolved issues from the previous phase should be high on the interventionist's list for the next point in time assessment. Unresolved issues from a previous phase will be included in the documentation review, and interviews for the next point time assessment will provide continuity between project phases to ensure that project failure points do not continue to go unaddressed.

How to intervene

I N THE LAST stage of collaborative intervention, your role is to present the findings of the assessment and to intervene in order to make necessary project changes.

Collaborative Intervention

The collaborative intervention process outlines **how** to intervene by presenting the findings of the assessment and working with the project team to develop an implementation plan to address the findings. Just as in the movies, the hero or heroine is aware that disaster is going to occur and must figure out how to stop it. The same is true for the enterprise project team. The project manager, a functional lead, or a key stakeholder may see the train wreck ahead, but doesn't know how to stop it. And that's where the collaborative part comes in. Who can stop a train wreck within your organization? Is it one person, two, an executive, a vendor, or a team composed of all of them? More than likely it is the team. And to stop the wreck or have the train change direction, you need the buy-in of multiple people and departments. It is the interventionist's job to bring the warning signs to the attention of the stakeholders, propose a solution, and facilitate its implementation.

How to intervene is discussed in section 3.

A funny thing happened on the way home – strategy and acquisition

A s Jenny pulled out of the restaurant, she couldn't help thinking about how the project would be structured. From what Bill mentioned, it sounded like the project has already gotten underway, and hopefully, it was still in the strategy phase.

If that is the case, Jenny thought, I will need to take a closer look at what FirstCorp is trying to accomplish by understanding both the business drivers and the problems the organization wants to solve. Obviously in this situation, FirstCorp has several objectives: to get on a supported platform, convert DataTech and outsource system support. I know Bill mentioned that Bobby's firm helped them develop a plan. I can't help but wonder if they conducted a detailed assessment or just facilitated some whiteboard sessions to come up with the strategy. That is where I need to start, Jenny decided. Did they conduct an assessment and to what level? That should provide me with some initial clues as to what I am dealing with.

Now Jenny found herself wondering if this strategy has been validated with Ted. She recalled that he was known to have his mood swings – and Bobby was afraid of him. In fact, as she turned things over in her mind, she was a little surprised that Bobby was still working with FirstCorp – he must have some incriminating pictures of Ted. The last project that Jenny could remember with CYA Partners involved was the BusinessWare post-implementation study. After the entire implementation was complete, Cindy, on behalf of Ted, had asked CYA Partners to conduct a study to validate that BusinessWare was the right system for FirstCorp, given all the mergers and evolving business requirements.

Once we got into the project, Jenny recalled, it turned out that all of us – including the project manager and the business owners and myself – had interpreted the purpose of the study differently. Our questions betrayed the confusion. Should we validate what we purchased? Should we look at new systems? Were there other systems and processes we missed? This disparity in viewpoints led to the debate as to what the project team was trying to accomplish.

These debates continued and were present at almost every project meeting. To Jenny, the solution seemed obvious – go back and validate what the purpose of the study is to make sure that the Ted's expectations are being met. The problem was the relationship with the CEO was becoming strained and Bobby was fearful of asking Cindy to go back to Ted to ask the purpose of the study. He didn't understand the importance of that one step which could validate the project, so it never happened. Therefore, the results fell short of expectations and the team was not given another chance to make necessary system improvements.

I better make sure that they validated expectations – starting at the top, Jenny decided. OK, that takes care of when to start: the strategy phase. Conducting the next point in time assessment will be tricky as it sounds like they have already made their procurement decisions. If this were a model implementation following the project lifecycle, I would recommend being involved in the procurement to make sure that the strategic plan and the needs assessment plan are translated into the software and services RFP to fulfill the business requirements. Since they are using existing providers with whom they have relationships, I'll still need to review their proposals and compare them back to the strategy documents and make sure that all groups and parties have been talked to.

Jenny started to laugh as she remembered an unbelievable story Bill had told her – a project at his former employer.

"As I remember it," Bill had said, "it was a situation where the business owners rushed to buy software without first validating the IT organization could support it. In this case, a financial team spent a good deal of time defining the business requirements and meeting with software vendors to purchase a new customer billing application. After a thorough evaluation and due diligence, the group proudly purchased the software – confident that they had made the right choice.

"Know what happened next? The team met with IT to install the product and start the implementation. To their horror, they discovered that the new software could only run on a technology platform *that was not supported by the IT organization. Someone failed to vali-date the system with the techies first."*

Well, that's a multi-million dollar bungle, Jenny thought, still crack-ing up about that situation as she pulled into her driveway. I'd better make sure that everyone who needs to be involved, is involved. It kind of reminds me of an intervention ...

After stopping the car, Jenny quickly typed her strategy and acqui-sition intervention notes into her smartphone and e-mailed them to herself.

Ballet, soccer, planning and design

*J*enny *unlocked the door to the house and let Toby out into the yard. The sheepdog wagged his tail in response and took off at a run. Jenny glanced at the hallway clock, noting that the kids would be home from school soon.*

Maybe a part time gig at FirstCorp wouldn't be so bad, she thought. It would still give me time to spend with the kids and shuttle them between their activities in the afternoon. Today is Tuesday, so Monica has dance from 4-6:00 p.m. and Jamie has soccer from 4:30-5:30 p.m. Luckily, the dance studio is fairly close to the soccer field. I may as well bring my laptop and work on the proposal for Bill since I'll need to wait for Jamie at soccer. In a busy life, multi-tasking is critical ... guess I'd better get used to it.

The door swung open promptly at 2:50 p.m. and the kids rushed in. Right on schedule, the school bus had dropped them off in front of the neighbor's house. "Hi Mom," Jamie tossed his backpack with on the table and headed to the fridge for a snack. Monica ran to Jenny, giving her a hug while pulling a drawing out of her pink backpack. "How was your day?" Jenny asked.

"I made a picture of a butterfly at school today for you, Mommy," Monica said, proudly handing Jenny her artwork.

"OK," Jamie said, already halfway to the basement to watch TV with a plate piled high with food.

"Hey," Jenny reminded him. "Only thirty minutes of TV – be ready to leave for soccer practice at 3:30."

"Mom ... 3:30?" Jamie shot back. "Practice doesn't start until 4:30!"

"Yes, but Monica has dance class at four o'clock and we have to drop her off first," she replied.

"Arrrrrrgh," Jamie moaned as if leaving a half hour early was the worst thing in the world.

"I'll be ready, Mommy," Monica said, trying to catch up with Jamie.

"Thanks, sweetheart."

At 3:30 p.m., Jenny loaded up the car, the kids buckled their seatbelts, and they headed to the dance studio. Parking in front of The World of Ballet, she walked Monica to the front door of the dance studio and opened it for her daughter. In her pink tights and black leotard, Monica instantly disappeared into a group of identically dressed little girls. Jamie looked bored as Jenny climbed back in the car to head to the soccer field. *Traffic is definitely getting heavier with the high school students getting out of class for the day and heading to afternoon activities,* she thought. Surprisingly, they arrived at the soccer field ten minutes early. Jenny found a shaded picnic table overlooking the soccer field and opened her laptop.

Jenny decided to focus on the next phases of the FirstCorp project, relying on her earlier notes from the drive home after lunch with Bill. *Tomorrow,* Jenny thought to herself, *I'll put the entire proposal together. I've already thought through the strategy and acquisition phases, so now it's time to think about assessing the project planning phase.*

Jenny began to write. "The planning phase is always interesting. For many parties, it marks the beginning of the project as the project team has expanded to include the project managers, the business owners, and subject matter experts, as well as vendors and integration consultants. During this phase, the project team is putting together the *project methodology, the project plan and the resource requirements, making the strategy more tactical.*

"An assessment at this stage will be important because the project has started and if there are gaps in the statements of work, project charters and detailed project plans, it is difficult to backtrack," she typed.

"Oh yeah, change management – talk about gaps," Jenny said out loud, as she banged away on her laptop. "Everyone always underestimates change management."

It was a cool fall afternoon and quite comfortable. Runners were jogging by on the trail around the soccer park. That would be me, Jenny thought. She usually used this time to sneak in a run while Jamie was practicing soccer, but not today. She needed to focus on this proposal. However, it still felt good to be outside.

As she watched the runners finish their laps, Jenny's thoughts drifted back to a recent project that didn't go so well. After she left FirstCorp, she had decided to strike out on her own as an independent consultant. Through a referral, the client hired her to be the project manager for a new system implementation. Seemed like a fairly straight-forward project – until the environment changed due to unforeseen events, including:

- *a lengthy delay between the procurement and start of the project*

- *unforeseen budgetary issues that required scope changes*

- *role changes in key project team members (sponsor and project manager) during the project*

In addition, expectations regarding the deliverables were not in alignment between the client and the software vendor. Both had different interpretations of the same wording in the statement of work. Although there was some discussion and agreement among the project managers, the differences in interpretation were never accepted by the team. The gap in expectations further widened when the client project manager left the organization for a new position and the team held their ground on their original interpretation. Too late to intervene in the failure issues that had persisted throughout the project lifecycle, the gap in expectations became too wide to bridge and the project resulted in unfulfilled expectations for the organization, vendor and the consultant – Jenny.

The thought of that project snapped her back to reality. Now she realized why Bill was so concerned about gaps. During the planning phase assessment, she definitely needed to make sure that she understood the expectations of each key player and acted before the gaps become too wide to bridge.

Jenny glanced at her watch, nearly 5:15 p.m. I've got a few more minutes before practice is over, Jenny thought, may as well keep going. "After the planning stage," her fingers flew over the keys, "the next logical assessment would be during the design phase. The design phase is important as it defines the system configuration and development. However, without controls in place, the design phase can be fluid because there is usually flexibility in scheduling as the project team may find that requirements were not fully understood during the earlier stages or there may be interdependencies that weren't uncovered until now – resulting in disconnects.

"Design disconnects often manifest themselves in additional meetings and requirements sessions pushing out the design phase end dates, but not changing the overall project time line. At the conclusion of this point in time assessment, it is appropriate to begin discussion about the go-live date. As difficult as these discussions maybe at this point in time, they will only become more difficult as the project progresses."

"Hey Mom, are you ready?" Jamie called, as he walked over to the picnic table.

"Sure son, just let me pack up and we'll go get your sister," Jenny said. She powered down her laptop and slid it into her shoulder bag. They walked to the car with her arm across Jamie's shoulders.

"So what's for dinner?" Jamie asked, his eyes lighting up.

"Good question." Jenny said, still too deep in thought about her project proposal to focus on the dinner menu. "I'm sure we have something at home – I know you must be starved after practice."

Acceptance, transition and a phone call from Tim

The next morning, with the kids off to school and armed with a second cup of coffee, Jenny sat down at her computer to continue working on the proposal for Bill. She'd only just begun when her cell phone rang. She recognized the number as coming from FirstCorp, and quickly answered. "Hello, this is Jenny," she said, as if she'd had been at work for hours now.

"Hey Jenny, this is Tim from FirstCorp." The voice had a familiar ring to it. "We worked together as project managers when I was with CYA Partners. How's it going?"

"Good, Tim. Long time, no talk," Jenny replied. "How've you been? I saw Bill yesterday and he told me that you've left the dark side and joined FirstCorp as an employee."

"That's right," Tim responded. "Jenny, Bill mentioned that you may be doing a project for us and I wanted to just touch base. I'm now running our PMO office and wanted to find out more about what type of work you may be proposing."

"Well," Jenny began, "Bill asked me to provide, oh ... what should it be called ... project quality assurance for the HR transformation project."

"Project QA?" Tim was quickly on the defensive. "You know, Jenny, that sounds a lot like IV&V – and my group handles IV&V."

"That's what Bill mentioned," Jenny felt her heart sink. This isn't good, she thought – and it's not even 9 o'clock in the morning. "Bill said, given all the players involved, he wanted someone from the out-side who could be objective."

"I'm not sure that I agree with that, but Bill is the boss." Tim stated flatly. "So give me an example of what you are thinking."

"Well, based on the conversation with Bill yesterday, I'm develop-ing a proposal to conduct several point in time assessments during critical stages in the system implementation lifecycle," Jenny explained. "For example, I'd conduct assessments during the strategy, acquisition, planning, design and ... "

Tim interrupted, jumping in with both feet. "I'm sure we don't need that, Jenny. We've got a strategy and our vendors are already lined up."

I thought for a moment. Obviously Tim is not comfortable with this and is starting to push back. I need to give him something more tangible.

"Tim, another example would be an assessment during the end of the development phase," Jenny said. "At this point in time, the project is either on track or not. If it's on track, I would look at change manage-ment, training and communications to see what we could do to increase the user acceptance of the system. And Tim," Jenny said with a laugh, "you have to admit, change management is always an issue at FirstCorp."

"Well, you got me there," Tim chuckled.

"And if the project isn't on track or development is behind, I'd look at what we need to do to adjust the project accordingly so that we aren't playing go-live chicken," she said.

"Go-live chicken ... what do you mean?" asked Tim.

"You're familiar with the game of chicken, right? Two people are advancing towards each other and the first one to move is the chicken," Jenny clarified. "It is also the preferred game for project teams that like to play with go-live dates."

"Jenny, I'm still not following you."

She tried again. "Ok, let's say we are on the HR Transformation project and we are behind schedule due to the sheer size of the upgrade and the complexity of the database. It's 7:00 am at the Monday *morning weekly meeting. Before we have even taken our seats, one of the project sponsors asks, 'Are we going to make the cut over date?' To which each of us respond, 'Yes, but there are issues with _____.' Tim, you fill in the blank. Training. User acceptance. Business process interruption. Resource allocation. Etc., etc."*

"So?" Tim waited.

"Because the project sponsor feels that the cut over date is more important than the readiness for the cut over, the end users will not be fully trained on the system," Jenny explained. "Sure, we can probably make the go-live date, but as a result, data entry errors will skyrocket and the personnel data will be compromised until the errors can all be identified and corrected. Now don't tell me you have never seen go-live chicken happen," Jenny said.

"OK, Jenny I get your point and I can see some value in what you're talking about," Tim admitted. "But I do want to warn you that things are different around here. There are rumors running rampant about budget cuts, layoffs, and even Bill."

"Even Bill?" Jenny went on the alert. "Tim, what do you mean by that?"

"Well, what I've heard from several sources is that he may not be around much longer," Tim said smugly, knowing he had just pulled the rug out from under Jenny.

"I don't believe that, Tim," Jenny said incredulously. "Ted simply cannot function without Bill. Besides, you and I both know that being COO has been Bill's dream job for years."

"Well, it all may just be rumor," Tim responded with a grin that Jenny could hear. "But I thought you should know before you get in too deep."

Jenny decided it was time to get back to work. "Tim, thanks for the heads up," she said, "and if I do come on board for this project, I hope that won't be an issue for you."

"It shouldn't be. I just wanted to find out more about what role you have," Tim said. "And I wanted to give you a feel for what's going on here inside FirstCorp."

"I appreciate that," Jenny said firmly. "Talk to you later, Tim."

"Have a good one, Jenny," Tim hung up.

Jenny walked out the kitchen door and sat on the porch in the crisp morning air for a few minutes to let her head clear. Toby trotted over to her and put his big, shaggy head on her knee, begging for a scratch. She obliged, running her fingers through his fur. *I just can't believe the rumors about Bill, Jenny thought, and Tim was really getting his jollies on that bit of gossip. But just in case it is true – I need to get this proposal finished and over to him as soon as possible.*

"Good boy, Toby," Jenny gave him one last pat and headed back inside to her computer. "I think I need one more point in time assessment before the go-live," she said to herself as she began to write where she had stopped when Tim called. During this final point in time assessment, she needed to ensure that everything is in place for system cut over or go-live weekend and that post production support is place.

"In addition," Jenny wrote, "we also need to ensure that the project is properly closed out, transitioned to operations, that the knowledge transfer from consulting resources has taken place and that deferred scope is prioritized. By the end of the project, the project team is ready to cut over and move on without having a plan for transition, support and phase II projects."

Alright, that should cover when to conduct the point in time assessment, she thought to herself as she finished the proposal. She looked at the wall clock ... thinking she might have time for a quick run and lunch before finalizing the proposal and sending it to Bill.

The proposal on the run

*N*othing like breaking away for a midday run to put things in perspective, *Jenny thought to herself as she pulled on her running shoes and hat in her driveway before starting up the hill. This was her traditional starting place for the three mile loop* that she has run hundreds of times over the last several years. The loop, as she called it, was a familiar jaunt up the hill leading out of the subdivision, past the middle school, weaving through a neighborhood, up and down another serious hill, turning onto a main road, passing the aromatic coffee shop, busy supermarket, numerous nail salons, and a dry cleaners. It finally looped back into her neighborhood with an easy finish down the hill to her house.

As she began to run, Jenny realized that the loop resembled her experience with projects. Projects usually start out going uphill, defining requirements, choosing software developing plans, getting everybody on the same page. At some point they level off, but there can be serious hills in the middle. If you do things right, the cut over should be a downhill glide to the finish.

But you can't predict the unknown, Jenny thought. There've been days when she struggled with the three miles due to extreme heat and humidity, how she was feeling, or the two cookies she popped down before she left the house. There have been other days when the run has been effortless and she felt like she could run the circuit a hundred times. Call it a runner's high ... whatever it is, she tried to capture that feeling so she could relive it on future days.

As Jenny's thoughts shifted to the proposal, things started to become clearer. What I am proposing is similar to the intervention that Bill conducted on the original BusinessWare implementation, she realized. But instead of one large, reactive intervention to avoid imminent disaster, Jenny was proposing to conduct a series of six smaller, proactive interventions to make sure that disaster never reared its ugly head.

The interventions would be conducted at six points in the project lifecycle where most failures occur:

Intervention #1: **Managing strategic expectations**.

This intervention would be conducted during the strategy phase during business case development or before the business case is presented for approval and funding.

Intervention #2: **Closing the procurement gap.**

This intervention would be conducted towards the end of the vendor selection process, before vendors are finalized and negotiations begin.

Intervention #3: **Aligning the troops.**

This intervention would be conducted towards the end of the planning phase after the initial drafts of the Project Charter, Detailed Project Plan and Change Management Plans have been developed.

Intervention #4: **The design disconnect.**

This intervention would be conducted towards the end of the design phase after the initial drafts of the System Design Documentation have been developed.

Intervention #5: **Evaluating acceptance.**

This intervention would be conducted towards the end of the development phase.

Intervention #6: **Transition and optimization.**

This intervention would be conducted towards the end of the testing and training phase before the system cut over.

Each of the six interventions was going to consist of the same seven steps:

1. Conduct expectations meeting.

The attendees will change depending on the phase of the project in which the intervention takes place.

2. *Review project documentation*.

Documentation will change based upon which project phase the intervention takes place within.

3. *Cross-reference documentation*.

Double-check the accuracy of each document against the other.

4. *Interview key participants*.

Find out what each individual is really thinking about the project and weigh the results against the overall project status.

5. *Determine areas of concern/recommendations*.

Focus in on those areas that are common areas of concern and develop ideas for corrective courses of action.

6. *Review findings with key participants*.

Discuss the results of the intervention process with key individuals involved.

7. *Final report/areas for follow-up*.

Hold a meeting to present the findings and determine areas for follow-up.

As Jenny rounded the corner towards home and headed down the hill, she realized today was one of those effortless runs. She felt good that she now had the structure for her proposal. All she had left to do was to estimate the total hours for the project and her billing rate to determine the total cost. Based on the structured intervention approach, she felt this was going to be a very reasonable proposal. Combined with the value proposition and Bill's comments from yesterday, she was confident in its acceptance.

Jenny walked into her house, downing a bottle of water while she popped a bagel in the toaster and jumped into the shower. After lunch, she finished proofing the proposal. All that was left was to come up with a name for the services that she would be providing. Jenny typed "Project Verification and Validation" – but then recalled both Bill's and Tim's comments about IV&V. She quickly changed the title to "Project Quality Assurance Services" and stared at the screen. Too many words, she thought as she began hitting the delete key. Jenny smiled for a minute and then saved the final document. She wrote an e-mail cover letter to Bill, attached the proposal, typed the title in the subject line and hit send.

Just to make sure that it was sent, she looked in her out box and saw the e-mail to Bill with the title in the subject line: "**Proposal for Project Assurance.**"

BECOMING AN INTERVENTIONIST

On the art of intervention

I T DOESN'T TAKE a rocket scientist to know that how you deal with people in difficult situations can be the most important component in project success. So far, you've learned about the critical intervention points and the point in time assessments that outline **when** to step in and **what** to look for at each step along the way.

In this section, we'll take a look at the art of the intervention – or the **how** – in the form of the attributes and behaviors of a successful interventionist as well as processes you can use for conducting project interventions.

Let's continue to follow Jenny on her journey to becoming an interventionist.

The coffee break

S o far so good, thought Jenny, as she confidently strode through the hallway at FirstCorp.

She had just concluded her review and cross-reference of the documentation for the first project assurance intervention. It was

10:00 a.m. and she was heading to the break room for her second cup of coffee.

Two weeks earlier, she had submitted her original project assurance proposal to Bill. As it turned out, the project team was further along than she had anticipated based on her brief discussion with Bill. By the time they received her proposal, the project team had already developed the strategy, finalized the contract with BigSI for hosting, upgrade consulting services and on-going support, and developed the detailed project plan.

Ideally, it would have been better to be involved from the very beginning, but large-scale implementation projects are never ideal. To make matters more interesting, the project that Bill had described to her over lunch was, in actuality, three projects:

1. Migrate the current HR system to BigSI for hosting and support
2. Upgrade FirstCorp's BusinessWare application to Version 8
3. Convert DataTech to FirstCorp's BusinessWare platform

Once her proposal had been accepted, Jenny learned that the system migration project was already underway and was informed that it wasn't within her scope for project assurance. She was to concentrate on the upgrade project and then, depending on how that went, she could be extended to assist with the conversion of DataTech's HR system to FirstCorp's BusinessWare platform.

All of this was fine with Jenny. The migration to the outsourcing platform was more of a technical project and she was happy not to be involved with it. However, she was concerned about the time line dependencies between the migration to BigSI and the upgrade project. She would have to have some involvement to make sure that the time lines synched up. No worries, she thought, I will speak to Bill. He will understand and clear the path for me to talk with BigSI.

In addition to the change in scope for Jenny, there was also a change in contact person. Bill was consumed with the merger, so he delegated the responsibility of working out the statement of work and contract to Tim. This was not Bill's first choice – he knew Tim wasn't thrilled about having Jenny on board, but in discussions with Brett, they agreed that by having Tim work with Jenny, it would help get him on board. Both Bill and Brett knew that Jenny had saved Tim from numerous missteps in the past when he was with CYA Partners. Deep down, Tim knew the value Jenny could bring to the project – he just didn't want to admit it. Adding insult to injury because funds were tight, Bill and Brett agreed that Jenny's fees would be coming out of the IT budget. Jenny's project would be charged to Tim's cost center.

As expected, working with Tim had a rocky start. Tim and Jenny went through a couple iterations of her project assurance proposal and fees before agreeing to the changes to her original proposal that included combining the first three assessments into one large assessment to address the strategy, acquisition and planning stages. The new plan was to conduct an initial larger intervention, present her findings and then conduct the subsequent interventions as she original proposed. Finally, they agreed to a rate reduction to fit the project budget. Tim begrudgingly accepted Jenny's revised proposal upon Bill's recommendation.

With the documentation review behind her, Jenny was deep in thought with her concerns as she poured hot coffee into her mug. The status of some of BigSI's key planning deliverables didn't seem to mesh with where they needed to be according to the planned cut over. She turned around and bumped into Tim.

"Whoa, watch it, Jenny!" Tim exclaimed, grabbing up paper towels to wipe her spilled coffee off of his white shirt.

"Oh my gosh - I am so sorry Tim!" Jenny apologized. "I guess I was lost in thought and didn't know you were right there."

"Damn, I just bought this shirt," said Tim, dabbing at his shirtfront.

"Tim, I am so sorry," Jenny repeated, trying to help with a fresh paper towel.

"Oh don't worry about it. I'll just deduct the dry cleaning costs from your fees," Tim replied, half jokingly.

Tim threw the crumpled paper towels into the trash can and grabbed a mug from over the sink. He poured himself a cup of coffee and glanced at Jenny, breaking the awkward silence.

"How are things going so far?" Tim said. "I assume you're settling in. Obviously you know where the coffee is."

Jenny smiled, relieved that the coffee drama was over. "It's like old home week, Tim. The running joke is that I'm like a bad penny: you guys just can't get rid of me."

"Sounds about right," Tim laughed. "No, seriously, I am just kidding."

Jenny smiled nervously. *I don't think he is kidding*, she thought to herself.

"Are we still on for 1:00 p.m. today in your office?" Jenny asked.

"Yep," Tim said, as he stirred heaping spoonfuls of sugar into his coffee. "I've asked Mark to join us, he will be the project lead for FirstCorp."

"Great, I saw that in the doc you provided, Tim." Jenny said, taking a sip of her coffee. "Any luck in setting up the call with the project manager from BigSI?"

"We can talk about that at one o'clock," Tim said, turning to leave.

"Good – and I am really sorry about the coffee," Jenny apologized for the third time.

There was no response as Tim walked away. Jenny wished she could start the morning over.

Interview with Tim and Mark

One o'clock arrived quickly. Given the situation with Tim, Jenny made sure that she was prepared and outside the door to his office a couple of minutes early, arriving the same time that Mark did.

Mark was a clean-cut, younger guy, one of Tim's project management protégés. From talking to a few of her former colleagues,

Jenny learned that Mark was well liked and known for his corny catch phrases and the latest buzzwords. Given his energy and attitude, Mark was also known to be very optimistic about his projects. A double-edged sword, his optimism kept the spirits of his project team members high, but it also led him to underestimate project complexities, level of effort and time lines.

"What's up Jenny, Jen-Jen-Jen?" Jenny heard as Mark approached. "You ready to light this candle?"

"I guess so," Jenny replied.

"Heard you dosed Tim with coffee this morning," Mark grinned conspiratorially. "Smooth move."

"Thanks, and this meeting should be interesting, too," she replied as Tim opened the door to his office.

"Should be," Mark responded.

They took their seats in the guest chairs as Tim sat down behind his desk and began typing on his keyboard.

"Give me a second," Tim said, without looking up, "I need to finish this."

While they waited for him to wrap up his e-mail, his cell phone rang.

"Oh – I need to take this, sorry," Tim said, as he answered the phone.

Fifteen minutes later, the meeting finally started.

"Thanks for taking time to meet with me today," Jenny began. "As you know, I've spent the last several days reviewing the needs assessment, project budget, and contract with BigSI and I do have some concerns."

"OK," Mark said, as Tim sat expressionless. "So what are they?"

"At this point in time, I'd expect to see the project charter, detailed project plan and change management plan," explained Jenny. "But what I have seen so far is basically a shell which looks like BigSI boilerplate."

"That's because it is boilerplate," Tim shot back. "Those deliverables are not due for a couple weeks, which is why I told you I did not think it made sense for you to start the project so quickly."

"Well, are you OK with this from BigSI?" Jenny asked.

"At this point, Jenny, I am," Tim spun in his desk chair around to the credenza and began to leaf through a stack of papers. "We had some additional 11th hour legal requirements regarding the hosting contract that pushed out some of the project dates and the deliverables. If you had reviewed the procurement documents, you would know this."

"Tim, I didn't see those documents," Jenny said, surprised. "Would you mind pointing out where that information is?"

"It should be in the notes from the hosting services procurement," Tim responded, his back still toward Jenny.

"I never got those documents, Tim. You said hosting services were out of my scope," Jenny shot back defensively. She could feel her heart starting to beat faster and her fist started to clinch. Hang on Jenny, she thought. This isn't going well. She needed to save this meeting before it turned into a brawl.

"I guess you're right," Tim said, turning around to face Jenny, knowing that he was getting under her skin.

"Listen Jenny," Mark interjected. "I'll get you those documents right after the meeting."

"Thanks, Mark," Jenny sighed.

"OK," Tim said flatly. "Besides the fact that you are already saying we are behind schedule, what else is on your mind?"

Jenny shifted in her chair. "I did not say you were behind schedule, I just said I was concerned about the status of some of the deliverables," she clarified. "But let's move on." Jenny started working down her list of predetermined questions, most of which Tim replied to with a series of one to two word answers: "Yes.", "No.", "Not really." or "You'll have to ask so and so."

As Jenny realized that Tim was not going to make this easy, she sensed it was time to wrap up the questions.

"So, at this point, do you have any additional concerns that I should be aware of?" Jenny asked.

"Not really," Tim responded, picking up his phone.

"Well, that wraps up my questions," Jenny said. "The only item I have left is the issue with BigSI. I really need to speak with their project manager."

Tim looked up for a moment. "I'm not sure why that is necessary, Jenny," he said. "You're going to have to convince me."

"In reviewing the project time line, I have a couple of concerns relating to BigSI," Jenny explained. "The first is connectivity. You know how long it takes to establish connectivity with all the security requirements on both sides, plus, if you are going to put in dedicated lines between FirstCorp and BigSI, that will take some time. Tim, you know what it is like working with the service providers and corporate security," Jenny went on. "If we do not have connectivity in place by the end of next month, we will have to push back the design sessions."

"Mark," Tim looked concerned for the first time. "I thought that connectivity was already established."

"Well, we've had some initial discussions, but work will not start for a couple weeks," Mark replied. "I thought that was sufficient. How hard can it be? It's not like we're building the space shuttle."

"Jenny's right on this one," Tim said firmly. "You haven't been around here long enough to fully grasp all that is involved. Let's discuss this in our meeting this afternoon."

"Good catch, Jenny," Tim said begrudgingly. "I knew we hired you for a reason. I'll send an e-mail introduction to the BigSI project manager. The two of you can take it from there."

"Is that it?" Tim asked.

"For now," Jenny said as she closed her portfolio.

"Let me know if you need anything else," Tim surprised them both with his offer.

"How about some coffee?" Mark joked as they stood up to leave Tim's office.

"I think I've had enough today," Tim grinned, looking down at the stain on his shirt.

"That was interesting," Jenny said to Mark as they walked toward the elevators. "What's up with his attitude?"

"I'm not sure," Mark said, suddenly serious. "Jenny, please don't take this the wrong way, but maybe you should ask yourself the same question."

"Whaa ...?" Jenny started to ask.

"Think about it," Mark said as he took a sharp right turn and went through the door to the stairwell to walk up the steps towards his cubicle.

"Ouch," Jenny felt a shooting pain in her side from Mark's comments. The elevator arrived and she got on, wondering what had just happened.

Granola with advice

Well, I guess it was a pretty tense meeting and I probably didn't do myself any favors, Jenny thought as she walked to the cafeteria for a bottle of water and a granola bar.

As she was paying for her snack, she saw Bill wrapping up a conversation with Mary at a table by the window. Noticing Jenny, he motioned her over to the table as Mary was walking away.

"Having a little snack with investor relations?" Jenny asked.

"I guess it looks that way," Bill grinned. "How is it going with you?"

"OK," Jenny said, despondently.

"Are you sure?" he asked. "You don't look so good."

"I wish I could say it wasn't so, but Tim and I had a little run-in," Jenny said, unscrewing the cap on her bottled water.

"Yeah, I heard about the coffee," Bill said chuckling. "I'm sure Tim knows it was an accident."

"That's not what I'm referring to," Jenny explained. "I just got out of a meeting with Tim and Mark – and it didn't go so well."

"Have a seat and tell me about it," Bill said as he pulled out the chair.

"It started on the wrong foot and went south from there," she sat down. "I laid out my issues and concerns with the project documentation and where BigSI is on several of their deliverables. I may have been a little too aggressive, given that they had delays to extended negotiations, which I was unaware of. Tim got defensive and basically shut down during my interview. On the good side, I did get across my concerns with the time line for connectivity. After I left the meeting, Mark told me I needed to adjust my attitude."

"Was he right?" Bill asked, once again knowing the answer.

"Probably," she responded slowly.

"Let's begin with the positive," Bill said. "Sounds like you made a good call on the connectivity issues, which means your analysis was solid. How did you figure it out?"

"Well, by analyzing the information in key project documents and cross-referencing it," Jenny replied. "Something was not clicking with the time lines, and I remembered what you had said about 'gaps'."

"Good – so you used your head," Bill praised her.

"Yep," she replied. "I like to think I'm analytical."

"Well, whatever you want to call it, that's still good," Bill answered. "You know, it always surprises me how project documents discuss **what needs to happen,** but don't address **how it is going to happen**. I've found that a major reason for this gap is that most project documents – such as charters and statements of work – are rarely developed from scratch. Most of the time, they are taken from previous projects and edited to suit the current project's needs. Another scenario for vague statements and project charters is that wording for a particular project area is simply copied from the vendor's proposal," Bill went on. "Keep in mind that when a vendor is responding to the proposal, particularly for an area that they have a corresponding weakness in, their response will be nonspecific. Look closely and you will see that they respond with what they are going to do versus how they plan to do it."

"I know exactly what you mean Bill," Jenny responded. "The tactic of describing **the what** versus **the how** is often used by vendors and project managers to obtain sign-off to documents or to get past a particular stage. This language can actually mislead the people who are reading the document because they assume the issues are being addressed just because there is a section in the document discussing what needs to happen. Without an analytical viewpoint, the how often goes unaddressed. By asking how something is going to occur, you should get a specific response. If you don't, the failure to get a specific response is a definite red flag."

"Glad we are on the same page," Bill replied. "Now let's talk about what didn't go so well."

"OK," Jenny swallowed hard.

"I know you need to be objective in your assessment," Bill reminded her. "Remember, that is one of the key reasons I wanted you involved in this project."

"I know, but it's difficult, Bill. I have a lot of valid concerns," Jenny explained. "You know we are really all on the same team."

"In order to be objective, Jenny," Bill said, "you've got to be fair, but have a healthy sense of skeptical realism."

"What do you mean by skeptical realism?" Jenny asked. "Sounds like one of Mark's buzzwords."

Bill laughed as he continued. "It's tricky, but in order to look objectively at the project from the outside in, you've got to have a healthy sense of both skepticism and realism. When you are conducting an assessment, especially the first assessment, more than likely you will be met with apprehension. It is human nature for people to feel threatened when their performance is being assessed.

"As a result, some project team members may overstate the progress or current state of the project, but you need to remain objective and skeptical enough to dig deeper into the answers instead of accepting them at face value. That lets you realistically assess the situation.

"By the same token, you have to be careful not to be too skeptical and assume that the project team isn't competent and that the project is a total disaster. For the most part, too much skepticism creates an antagonistic relationship with the project team that is counter-productive."

"Which is what happened today," Jenny said slowly, as if the shades on the window were suddenly opened, letting in the light.

"Exactly," Bill explained. "This is why you must balance your objectivity with skepticism and realism. You know that understanding the environment surrounding the project team is critical to building the trust necessary to develop collaborative solutions for live project issues."

"Collaborative solutions?" queried Jenny. "What does that mean?"

"I use the word collaborative because one person alone can't troubleshoot and solve a group's problems. It has to be the group that agrees on the issues, seeks out the best solution and puts it into place," Bill responded.

"When you put it like that," Jenny said thoughtfully, "maybe I did start a little too early in assuming that the project was already in jeopardy because key documents and deadlines have been missed. If I had done a little more due diligence, I would have realized that the additional contract negotiations pushed back the start date."

"Objectivity trumps assumption every time," Bill replied, smiling at her, "and a little diplomacy wouldn't hurt either."

Diplomacy? Jenny thought. Hey, this isn't the United Nations.

Bill continued. "Diplomacy is critical to creating the collaborative environment for the intervention and helps you to communicate effectively in coaching the team to address and resolve issues. Think about your meeting. You had the knowledge and analytical ability to identify the gaps in the project, but you went into the meeting with Tim and Mark with the assumption that they would just listen and accept what you were saying. Even if your assessment of the situation is correct, without diplomacy, you'll have little luck in facilitating a collaborative solution, much less implementing it.

"Furthermore, this will be especially important if you get involved with DataTech. Because of the dynamics of the culture and relationships within the organization, among departments, and between the vendor and the client, your ability to negotiate will be tested."

Negotiate? Jenny thought to herself. He really does think this is the U.N.

"Look, I know you may be skeptical, but at the heart of diplomacy is the ability to negotiate," Bill said earnestly. "It is easy for someone to act diplomatically and build congenial relationships, but oftentimes these relationships are only on the surface. To be truly diplomatic, the relationship must evolve from platitudes to mutual trust and respect. Keep in mind that during an intervention, you will be viewed with skepticism. Using diplomacy, it is your job to overcome that skepticism and build a respectful working relationship. Once mutual trust and respect have been established, the parties can work together to negotiate solutions.

"You know, Jenny, I've been doing this a while. From what I have seen, successful consultants are often the most diplomatic. In many cases, a consultant may have similar experiences and expertise to the client. However, the client is bringing in the consultant to help solve the problem that they are unable to solve themselves. This usually happens because communications have broken down. The consultant's role is similar to a diplomat negotiating issues between opposing nations: it is to gain consensus and to help negotiate a solution while using their own experience to establish credibility as an expert. Without diplomacy, your ability to facilitate and build consensus for the solution will fail."

Bill leaned back in his chair. "Does that make sense?"

"Sure." Jenny nodded her head, still thinking about what Bill had just said.

"I need to get going," Bill pushed his chair back and stood up. "I have a 3:00 p.m. meeting with Ted."

"Good luck with that one," Jenny replied, asking, "Were you having pre-meeting with Mary?"

"Somewhat," Bill grinned. "Hang in there, Jenny, tomorrow is a new day."

Running with it

Talking to Bill made me feel better, Jenny thought to herself as she walked back to her desk. She decided to call it a day.

She packed up her laptop, grabbed her keys and headed for the parking deck. The emotions of the day –dosing Tim with coffee, the meeting, Mark's comment, and talking to Bill had worn her out, and she still had an evening of kid's activities ahead of her. Hopefully, she would have a chance for a quick run during Jamie's soccer practice. She needed to decompress.

When Jenny finally pulled into her driveway, she found the kids inside. Her husband, Jeff, was working at home today - one of the perks of his flexible schedule. She opened the door to his office to say hello and was shooed away. Oops, I didn't realize he was on a conference call, Jenny thought to herself. Sudden, unexpected interruptions – definitely one of the hazards of working from home.

Jenny hurried the kids to get ready for dance and soccer. As always, Monica was already in her tutu and had her bag packed by the door. Jamie was lying on the couch and eating pretzels while watching TV – still in his school clothes.

"Let's go, Jamie, you need to get ready," Jenny called.

"Mom, I got two more minutes," he sassed back.

Technically that was true, but since it will take Jamie an extra five minutes to find his cleats and shin guards in the mountain of clothes on the floor in his room, he will need those two minutes and five more to get ready, Jenny thought. She took advantage of it and changed into her running clothes and laced up her shoes.

After the mad dash out of the house, two trips from the end of the driveway back to the house to get Jamie's water bottle and soccer ball, and dropping Monica off at the dance studio, Jenny and Jamie arrived at the soccer park. Jamie took off to join his teammates on the field. Jenny walked to the gravel trail that meandered through the trees around the perimeter of the park, did some quick stretches, put her headphones and started off on her run.

She selected an aggressive music play list. She needed to burn off some steam.

I need to change my attitude? Jenny thought as she hit the half-mile marker and started up the hill by the soccer fields. Who do they think they are? I just saved their butts again.

"Well, I guess Tim and Mark are the clients," she said out loud. Maybe she should have been more strategic instead of rushing into that meeting with guns a-blazing.

She could almost hear Bill's comments. "Strategy is what separates an intervention process from a normal project audit, being strategic means having a plan, method, or series of maneuvers for obtaining a specific goal or result."

Strategy. It makes perfect sense, Jenny thought as the music blared in her ears and she rounded the corner into her second loop around the park.

Given her day, it was impossible for Jenny not to think of strategy in military terms. Almost all definitions of strategy refer to warfare, battle or competition. And frankly, there were similarities to her project. Just as a general or competitor must understand his or her opponent, Jenny realized that she must understand the players involved in order to implement the recommendations and action plans. She was naïve to think that the team would just accept and implement her recommendations automatically. Obviously, they put up some resistance.

Jenny needed to understand the dynamics of the environment, the sources of power, the decision making process and their collective impact on the implementation of the recommendations. She must not only build solutions, she also needed to develop and implement the plan for communicating the problems and resulting solutions, otherwise this project will be just another project audit.

Tim and Mark both knew that Jenny would find and present any gaps and deficiencies in their project. It wasn't their fault – they were both good project managers, but sometimes it isn't possible to cover everything in the time frame available. Sometimes they may not have the breadth of experience to identify gaps, such as the case with the connectivity issue. It was Jenny's job to find the gaps, but she needed to expect resistance, pushback or even an unwillingness to recognize and resolve the gaps.

Jenny needed to have a better strategy to build consensus among project decision makers that the solutions are necessary and to get them to agree to the approach to implement the solutions. She may need to hold more informal meetings, or where sensitive issues are involved, have private meetings with key stakeholders before presenting her recommendations and putting people on the spot.

Not only do I need to be objective, analytical and diplomatic, Jenny thought, I need to have a strategy as well. She finished her final lap, grabbed the water bottle and towel from the car and walked over to pick up Jamie.

He grinned at her, "Hey Mom, can we stop and get a smoothie on the way home?"

"I don't know son, I'm kind of full," Jenny replied with a smile. "I just had a big slice of humble pie."

"Did you get me a piece?" Jamie asked.

"No, sweetheart. It doesn't taste very good," Jenny laughed. "We'll stop for smoothies. We can get your sister one as well."

Today is a new day

Bill's words echoed in Jenny's head as she got the kids off to school and started navigating the drive to the office. At the red light, she read an e-mail on her smartphone from Anil, the project manager from BigSI. He was asking her for a 10:00 a.m. phone call to discuss the connectivity issues. *At least Tim followed through on setting up the call for me,* Jenny thought.

She pulled into the parking lot at the coffee shop to fill up her travel mug. Part of her new strategy was to avoid the break room and she was going to need an extra cup of coffee to address the day. Jenny had the 10:00 a.m. call with Anil and a 4:00 p.m. meeting with Bill, Brett and Tim to review her preliminary findings. She was hoping to have more time to compile her report, but given both Bill's and Brett's schedule, it was either meet at four o'clock today or wait two weeks – too late to be effective.

Jenny was fine with the time frame when Bill and Brett agreed that she could put some summary slides together for the meeting today and deliver the final report by next Monday.

She got to her desk about 9:00 a.m. and started to prepare for the call with Anil. Jenny now had two main concerns for Anil. The first was timing: would there be connectivity from BigSI's hosting center back to FirstCorp in time to conduct the design session?

Her second concern was migration. If DataTech was eventually going to migrate to the BusinessWare Version 8, shouldn't they be involved in the design sessions as well, especially given the size and complexity of the business rules? It made complete sense to Jenny, otherwise they would have to adapt to FirstCorp's business processes or further customize the system. DataTech needed to be involved to determine the gaps between the two merging entities.

Precisely at 10:00 a.m., her cell phone rang. "Hello, this is Jenny," she said.

"Jenny, this is Anil from BigSI," a deep, male voice said. "How are you today?"

"I'm fine – and you?" Jenny replied.

"Doing well, although it is still early here on the West coast," Anil chuckled. "But you get used to it."

"Oh my," Jenny exclaimed. "I didn't realize how early it is for you – do you want to reschedule for later in the day?"

"No of course not, I'm awake now," Anil responded. "Tim tells me that you're helping out with project quality assurance."

"You could say that," Jenny said.

"Tim did mention the connectivity issues. You know, we had brought that up to Mark as well, but he dismissed it," Anil related. "I'm glad you've resurrected it."

"Thanks, Anil." Jenny relaxed a little. "When do you think connectivity will be established?"

"You realize that it's hard to say exactly, I'm thinking six weeks at minimum, but more than likely eight weeks," Anil estimated. "It isn't as much the result of BigSI or FirstCorp schedules as it is the third party carrier."

"I understand," Jenny said. "But design sessions are scheduled to start in four weeks."

"I know, but there isn't much we can do about the third party carrier," agreed Anil. "One idea that we had was to have the FirstCorp team come out to our location for the design sessions. We already have the systems up and running here and could conduct the session in our classrooms."

"Well, that is a good idea," Jenny said thoughtfully. "Thanks for the suggestion."

"Anil, I have another issue as well," said Jenny. "Believe me, I'm not trying to ambush you – but this just came to me on the drive to work this morning."

"OK," Anil said warily, "what is it?"

"Well, it's regarding the three stages of the project," Jenny explained. "Obviously the first stage, migrating the environment to BigSI, is already underway. But it seems to me that DataTech should be involved in the design sessions to make sure that the system is designed to meet any unique requirements they have. This could prevent any potential rework or surprises in the third stage of the project."

"That makes sense," Anil replied. "I already know that they want some involvement. Actually, we could conduct the design sessions at DataTech because they already have connectivity to us. We could probably set up their access to the design environment in a matter of days."

"That sounds like a good compromise, Anil," Jenny responded. "I'm meeting with Bill, Brett and Tim later today and will bring it up with them. Not sure what will come of it, but I appreciate the suggestion and your willingness to come up with alternative solutions."

"No problem, Jenny, just let me know how it goes," Anil said. "I'm sure we will have to tweak the statement of work a bit."

"Speaking of which, how are the planning deliverables coming?" Jenny asked quickly.

"Good, we will have them to you next Wednesday – two days ahead of the revised schedule," chuckled Anil.

"Great, I look forward to reviewing them next week," Jenny said. "If you have any questions or need anything else, just give me a call."

"Will do, Jenny," Anil replied, "and let me know about the design sessions."

"As soon as I have a decision, I'll be in touch," Jenny said as she hung up the phone.

That went better than expected, Jenny thought as she started developing her strategy for the meeting this afternoon.

Meeting prep

Jenny worked through the lunch hour developing her material for the afternoon meeting.

Taking a break, she walked over to Tim's office to give him an update of the conversation with Anil. She was realizing that sharing her thoughts with him before the planned session at 4:00 p.m. would help build his trust in her efforts.

"Do you have a moment for a quick update?" Jenny leaned against the doorway to Tim's office.

"Yeah, sure," Tim walked over to his conference table and pulled out a chair for her. Jenny explained her concerns and related the subsequent call with Anil. Tim nodded throughout her narrative and agreed with her about the need to include DataTech in the design sessions. He also liked Anil's suggestion about conducting the design sessions at their location.

"We may have to secure some additional funding to cover the travel costs," Tim said thoughtfully. "But we could pull it from the phase III budget since DataTech is involved."

"Tim, I knew you'd find a way," Jenny smiled. She rose to leave. "I'll see you at 4:00 p.m."

Jenny returned to her desk. The only thing she had left to do was to summarize the overall status of the project. She bent to the task. An hour later, she finalized her slides.

To summarize and communicate her findings, Jenny developed a three-level rating system:

Level 1 - All systems go: remain vigilant

- Good organizational knowledge and some minor gaps in overall process or methodology (minor gaps in project documents-needs assessment/requirements analysis)

- Key decisions made in a timely manner. Proven issue resolution process

- No unforeseen events / potential realization of low impact risk

- Resource issues can be resolved within contingency budget

Level 2 - Proceed with caution: potential time bombs

- Some lack of organizational knowledge resulting in a gaps in overall process or methodology (some gaps in project documents-needs assessment/requirements analysis)

- Some key decisions in limbo or some uncertainty regarding the issue resolution process

- Potential for some minor unforeseen event / realization of moderate impact risks

- Resource issues require additional resources not to exceed 10% of original budget, plus contingency. Issues may include:
  - unexpected change in project resources due to improper planning
  - additional costs
  - missed or added scope
  - not enough resources or not enough of the right resources

Level 3 - Danger ahead: immediate action required

- Significant lack of organizational knowledge resulting in a major gap in overall process or methodology (no needs assessment/requirements analysis)

- Significant decisions in limbo or lack of issue resolution process

- Potential for major unforeseen event / realization of high impact risks.

- Resource issues require significant additional resources exceeding 20% of original budget, plus contingency. Issues may include:
    - unexpected change in project resources due to improper planning
    - additional costs
    - missed or added scope

- Not enough resources or not enough of the right resources

Jenny finished the last slide and the last sip of her now cold coffee. She glanced at her watch – it was 3:45 p.m. Based on her initial findings, she believed that the project was at Level 2. Some things were going well, but potential time bombs existed in the form of connectivity and DataTech's involvement in the design session. Interestingly, both of these findings were technically out of Jenny's scope, as these were events that would not occur for the phase of the project that she was assigned to, but in the first and third phase of the project. However, because of the dependencies and impacts on her phase of the project, she had the responsibility to bring them up.

The meeting was held in the executive conference room, the same conference room that Jenny had met with Cindy during the original implementation. Everything looked the same, except for a few updated awards and some new faces in the executive suite, notably Bill, the COO, and Brett, who was CIO.

Waiting for the meeting to begin, Jenny noticed a lot of buzz going around the executive suite. That was not unusual. What was unusual was the fact that everyone was in Ted's office.

Finally, the meeting started, twenty minutes late. Jenny noticed that Brett looked stressed while Bill looked relaxed – maybe too relaxed.

"OK, let's get started," Bill said. "Jenny?"

"Thanks, Bill," Jenny said as she passed out paper copies of her slide presentation. "I know you all are busy, so I've summarized the main issues."

As usual, Jenny started with the background of the project. She quickly overviewed how they had gotten to this point, what documentation she had reviewed and with whom she had spoken. Because Jenny had given Tim a heads-up earlier in the day, he wasn't apprehensive because he was already on board with some of her recommendations. She discussed the project status, warning of the potential problems that could arise from the connectivity issue if DataTech was not included in the design sessions. Jenny then offered the proposed solutions giving Tim and Anil full credit for coming up with the recommendation to move the design session to DataTech.

The presentation was well received. Brett took the action item to get in touch with DataTech regarding their involvement in the design sessions. Jenny was feeling good about her presentation as well as the project until Bill asked Tim and her to stick around for a minute.

"Tim and Jenny, I need to mention one thing before we wrap up," Bill began as the room cleared. "As you know, mergers are complicated. As a result of the recent merger with DataTech, we are a bit top heavy at the leadership level. Obviously, it makes sense for Ted to continue as CEO, but the Board feels we need to make room for Angie, the CEO of DataTech, as part of the united company moving forward. She is quite talented. I've been offered two choices: a new position to head up the European operations or accept a package.

"Given where I am at this time in my career and the size of the package, I am opting for that. I informed Ted and the executive team of my decision in the previous meeting – which is why we were late getting started with this one," Bill finished.

"Wow," Jenny sputtered, shocked. "Congratulations, I guess?"

"Thanks Jenny, it really is a good thing," Bill smiled. "I've already had a few job offers, I'm going to take some time off to think about what I want to do next. FirstCorp will be issuing a press release tomorrow with the changes, but I wanted you both to hear it from me."

"We appreciate hearing this from you," said Tim. "I guess that explains why Brett looked stressed."

"Yes," Bill agreed. "Brett knew he had an ally in me because I understand technology. He may have his hands full with Ted and Angie."

"When is your last day, Bill?" Jenny asked.

"Today," Bill replied. "It's best for me to exit quickly so the company can move on. There is a safety net however; I'm still on retainer if the company needs me for anything. From what I can tell, Angie is quite capable."

"Good luck, Bill," Tim walked over to Bill and shook his hand.

"I guess we'll see you around," Jenny grinned, "at least I hope so."

"Feel free to call me if you need anything, you know how to reach me," Bill said as we turned to leave the conference room. His cell phone chirped, and Bill answered it, holding up his hand to stop us from walking away.

"Hey, Brett," Bill said as he turned his attention to the phone.

A moment later, Bill hung up. "Brett just spoke with Dave, the CIO at DataTech, and he is good with conducting the fit-gaps at their location. Just give his assistant a call and she will connect you with the right people," Bill grinned. "I hope you guys have some warmer clothes."

"Warmer clothes, what do you mean?" Jenny asked. "DataTech's headquarters are just across town."

"Well, headquarters are across town, Jenny," Bill replied, "but the HR and system support teams are located just outside Chicago near the Wisconsin border."

That's news to me, Jenny thought. Great. First Bill's leaving and now I find out I have to travel to the frozen tundra of the Midwest.

Mastering the fundamentals

The last couple of weeks have flown by, Jenny thought, as she waited on the dark runway, hoping the plane would take off before the thunderstorms rolled in. Travel just wasn't the same these days: smaller planes, crowded flights and fewer options.

It was Monday night and Jenny was flying into Milwaukee. She planned to stay in the business suites by the airport and get up early to drive south across the Wisconsin/Illinois border to DataTech's service center. The design sessions hosted by DataTech were starting to wrap up and she planned to attend a few of the remaining sessions. In addition to her proposed assessment activities of reviewing documentation and conducting interviews, Jenny decided it would be a good idea to sit through a few of these meetings to witness the tone of the project team members and understand how the dynamics were playing out.

As she tried to get comfortable on the plane, she knew that she had her work cut out for her. Mark had mentioned that DataTech's team had been tough to deal with and installed a governing committee that made all of the decisions as a group. Great, she thought, instead of potentially one indecisive, difficult person, I might have to deal with a whole team of them. She definitely needed a strategy going into this situation.

As the plane accelerated and lifted off from the ground, Jenny's thoughts drifted back to what she learned from the first intervention about being analytical, objective, diplomatic and strategic. However, for that intervention, Jenny had one advantage: Tim and Bill knew her and the caliber of her work – and that helped to establish her credibility. *These people don't know me from Eve,* Jenny thought, *so I need to take this into consideration and work to achieve their trust.*

From the moment I walk in the door tomorrow, I plan to open my ears and listen, she thought. *I've seen it a hundred times.* In fact, CYA Partners is famous for this. They would send in consultants who believed that they had the answers to the all the problems before they walked in the door. Their experience (or lack thereof) gave them the egotistic ability to think they could recognize the same situations in different environments. But the truth of the matter is that there are no two implementations alike. There are unique factors, different influences and distinct pressures that allow no categorization of a project – other than the type of technology being implemented.

Frankly, Jenny was often surprised by how many people don't actually listen to conversations or what people are trying to communicate to them. They're too busy listening to their own thoughts in formulating a response or they just want to hear themselves talk or even to get the last word. Jenny had even seen consultant jam piles, where a room full of consultants trying to impress their clients kept the conversation going, each trying to out-do the other and have the last word. At the end of the day, they usually talked so much that they confused everybody and made the situation worse.

From all the indications, Jenny knew she needed a different approach. *I am going to focus on being humble and putting myself in the other person's shoes,* she thought, *so I can really understand what they are saying.* Plus, if she could sit back, listen and observe the behaviors and dynamics, she could develop her strategy as the day progressed.

Jenny woke with a start when the plane jolted upon touching down. Glancing at her watch, she realized how late it was, and given the long day behind her, that she must have dozed off on takeoff. After *wiping her eyes and stretching, she had a moment of clarity regarding her strategy for the week.*

The only way I am going to be successful and figure this situation out is to master the fundamental behaviors of listening, understanding, compromise and humility, Jenny thought, as she grabbed her bags and headed to the hotel.

Lay low and observe

AFTER EATING BREAKFAST *and driving more than an hour to the client site, Jenny walked into DataTech's lobby and asked for Mark at the front desk. As a result of her findings about connectivity and DataTech's involvement in the design sessions, both the FirstCorp and BigSI project teams have been traveling to northern Illinois for the design sessions. Although most of the team was not opposed to travel, the fact that winter was just beginning did not make it any better for the FirstCorp team, which was located in the deep South while the BigSI team hailed from southern California.*

"Jenny, Jen-Jen-Jen," Jenny heard as Mark walked out to the front desk.

"Hey Mark, how is it going?" Jenny said brightly.

"Can't complain. So what do you think of these digs?" Mark asked.

"Interesting," Jenny replied as they walked past the reception area. Despite its name, DataTech's service center did not project the image of a technology company. The service center itself appeared to be a converted retail big box store. All the cash register lanes and shopping aisles had been replaced with rows of office cubicles, but some of the original paint on the large walls still indicated shopping departments – house wares, toys and automotive.

"The project team is grouped over here in sporting goods," Mark laughed as they walked through the aisles to Jenny's temporary office.

As she approached the project team group, Jenny recognized familiar faces from FirstCorp seated at their temporary workstations. She was greeted with a lot of welcoming smiles – they were happy to see a familiar face as well.

As the morning passed talking to the team, Jenny learned that while the team felt that the sessions were productive, there was definitely some resistance and few turf wars going on. On the positive side, the consultants from BigSI were knowledgeable and had good product experience – which was refreshing as this wasn't always the case. On the negative side, the team was tired from the travel and didn't like their hotel or the local restaurants in the area. Oh well, not much I could do about that, Jenny thought to herself. Good thing I'm only here for this week.

Jenny had fifteen minutes until the next design session was to begin. She unpacked her laptop, hit the restroom, and grabbed a cup of some sludge that slightly resembled coffee. Along the way, she ran into Anil, the project manager from BigSI.

"Anil, it's great to meet in person," Jenny said warmly. "How is it going?"

"There's the good and the not so good to report," responded Anil. "What do you say we discuss what's happening later on?"

Jenny and Anil decided to get together towards the end of the day to catch up.

She took her seat in the back of the room, trying just to lay low and observe the meeting. Today's topic was a technical discussion on conversions and interfaces. In addition to business users, the meeting attendees included the developers from both companies. This should be interesting, Jenny thought. Technical people like to focus on the details and often try to drive the business processes with the limitations of the technology or the programs, rather than adjusting the technology to meet the requirements of the business processes. In addition, FirstCorp was not used to operating in an outsourced environment. That change alone would require some alterations in thinking as well as roles and responsibilities.

This design session was being led by Anil. He began with a discussion of the data fields that would have to be converted or combined in the new release. There was obvious discomfort – both about the fact that each organization had a different way of doing things and would have to use common tool sets. What Jenny found interesting was that DataTech, because they had been outsourced to BigSI, had more standardized tools and technologies in place, whereas FirstCorp still used outdated programs that were custom developed to meet their needs in the 1990s. Because these old tools still worked and were behind the scenes, the technology wasn't upgraded over time. Due to Jenny's history with FirstCorp, she was very familiar with the tools as well as the technical team's unwillingness to let go. However, the BigSI platform was more advanced and the DataTech team seemed to have a good grasp of its capabilities.

The design session dragged on for an extra half hour as a few of the FirstCorp technical people took everyone down a rabbit hole trying to explain their specific needs for the custom tools. It was becoming obvious that these folks really didn't want to change and were going to have trouble functioning in the new environment. Finally the meeting ended. Jenny sneaked out of the room before getting dragged into another detailed discussion. Plus, she was getting hungry.

Sweet potato fries and FirstCorp's issues

Jenny had scheduled a lunch meeting with Maureen, the project manager from DataTech. Maureen was a friendly, midWestern woman who insisted that they try a local restaurant for lunch to get a feel for the town. They ended up at Milligan's, a local tavern and sandwich shop that happened to be owned and operated by the husband of one of the DataTech project team members. According to Mark, it was the only decent restaurant in town and therefore was pretty crowded at lunchtime. Maureen and Jenny found a couple of seats at a bar top table and ordered iced teas and sandwiches.

"So, I hear that you have a history with FirstCorp," Maureen started, sipping her tea.

"Well, you could say that," Jenny responded. "I was a project manager at FirstCorp for the original system implementation before going independent as a consultant."

"Interesting," Maureen observed thoughtfully. "So what are your thoughts on the project so far?"

"First impressions? It seems like things are on track, but I still have some concerns," Jenny replied. "The conversion and interfaces meeting was very interesting."

"To say the least," Maureen responded wryly. "We may have the advantage in the technical areas as we are familiar with BigSI and the hosting environment."

"How is that going?" Jenny queried. "You know there's a lot of chatter about their service levels."

"You're right, at first it was a bit rocky," Maureen agreed. "We had expected them to know our business immediately, so there were a lot of growing pains. But now that they know us, things are pretty smooth. That isn't to say that there are not issues from time to time, but we are able to work them out. Anil does a great job of making sure that if the issues are on their side, they get resolved. He also lets us know when something is our fault, which happens too."

The sandwiches arrived and they began to eat.

"I am glad to hear it," said Jenny, between bites of her chicken salad on whole wheat. "I just think the FirstCorp team is apprehensive of the whole relationship. You know they have been doing things themselves for some time now with the same team. Some of these folks have been in the IT department at FirstCorp for over 20 years. Old-timers often have a rough time dealing with change."

"I can certainly see that," said Maureen. She dabbed at her mouth with her napkin before leaning forward on the table. "Jenny, you know we are having a lot of discussions about why we can't do something instead of how things could look in the future. The weird thing is, we are already doing what they say we cannot do, but it seems as if we are speaking a different language."

"OK," Jenny said. "Obviously we are going to have some things that we need to work out with the technical folks. What else are you worried about?"

Maureen hesitated, chewing a bite of her corned beef sandwich. "Well, don't take this the wrong way. I know that technically we are being acquired by FirstCorp, but our business processes are more advanced and our use of the system is more functional than First-Corp's," Maureen said. "We have pushed many of the functions out to the end users through self-service functionality. FirstCorp is still using centralized administrators. Bottom line? If we follow FirstCorp with the system conversion, I feel like we will be taking steps backward."

"Interesting," Jenny commented. "Have you communicated this to the project's executive committee?"

"Somewhat, but as you know it is complicated environment given the politics involved," Maureen said, finishing her tea. "I've brought it up to my manager, Mel, but he's definitely reluctant to bring it up to the executive committee."

"Maybe that is something I can help with," Jenny mused.

"Oh, I doubt it," Maureen replied.

"Well, I'm going to try anyway," Jenny smiled. "Thanks for introducing me to Mulligan's. That sure was a great sandwich and you're right, you can't beat the sweet potato fries."

"Glad you liked it, Jenny," Maureen grinned. "Ready to head back to the sporting goods department?"

"Sure," Jenny laughed. "Let's grab a cup of coffee to go. Given the size of my lunch, I think I'm going to need it."

Green isn't always green

The afternoon went by quickly as Jenny typed up her notes from the technical design session and lunch with Maureen. Around 3:00 p.m., she sat in on the weekly project management meeting and issue log discussion. Based on the status, it sounded like everything was pretty much on track. However, the team was starting to miss a few deadlines as additional requirements were being identified and document review deadlines were slipping. Even though the additional requirements would require more meetings, the project team felt they could squeeze them in. Jenny made some quick notes for her meeting with Anil.

After the meeting, Anil and Jenny stayed in the room to catch up.

"It is good to finally have a chance to catch up face-to-face," Jenny smiled at Anil. "Thanks again for your suggestion to have the design sessions here. It has certainly made a difference in keeping the project on track."

"I don't think my suggestion for a change in venue won me any friends at FirstCorp," Anil chuckled. "As you've probably heard, the natives are getting restless and want to go home."

"Oh yeah, I got an earful first thing this morning," Jenny grinned. "But I also think that everyone knows, deep down, that this is the best way to work through the design phase of this project. It was an interesting meeting this morning, Anil. Have the dynamics been the same for all the sessions?"

"Somewhat," Anil observed. "It is difficult for FirstCorp to grasp some of the concepts and how DataTech could be ahead of them in terms of the system implementation."

"Yes," Jenny agreed. "Maureen expressed some of the same concerns during lunch today."

"Good," Anil said. "I'm glad you two had a chance to catch up. Maureen has good ideas, but often gets run over by Mark and Tim."

"Yeah, I can see that," Jenny replied. "So, from this last meeting, it sounds like additional requirements are popping up and extending the time line."

"Well that's not unusual, now that we are getting into the details," Anil responded.

"No, not at all," Jenny concurred, "but I am concerned as to why some of the deliverable review deadlines are being missed."

"It's not that everyone isn't working hard, it's just that we are short on functional people," declared Anil. "This project requires a new way of doing things and many of the project team members are not comfortable with the change. Those people leading the change almost have to be involved with everything to make sure that the team does not revert back to the old way of doing things. Frankly, it is spreading them too thin.

"Also, we have a lot of people assigned to the project part time. They still have their real jobs to deal with. This is not so much the case for FirstCorp because they are traveling up here and cannot get sucked back into other issues as easily, but we definitely have issues with the DataTech staff getting pulled out of meeting to fight fires."

"Interesting ..." Jenny mulled this information over.

"Is it?" Anil sighed. "I bet if you went back and reviewed the project org chart you will see that 70% of the people listed are either being pulled into their other jobs or are not effective – meaning they are the wrong people for the role. The other 30% is doing the lion's share of the work."

"Yes," Jenny commented. "I noticed the same thing when I cross-referenced the resource loading on the project plan to the project charter. Any suggestions?"

"Yeah," Anil snorted. "Get more people. Backfill people on the team or bring in more consultants. It is pretty obvious. The real problem is getting Tim and Mark to acknowledge that this is a problem."

"Maureen said something similar, Anil, that even though you've identified a few problems, you cannot get them resolved," Jenny dug deeper. "What's up with the executive committee?"

"They meet once a month and, up to this point, there have not been many issues," Anil explained. "Overall, the project is still green on the dashboard. They see that color green and think everything is on track. Plus, it is difficult to get the issues on Tim's agenda. He would rather fix these things himself than bring them up to the EC. The problem is that organizationally, he is not in a position to do much. Maybe you can help."

"I am going to try," Jenny heard herself say for the second time today. "Anil thanks for your time. This has been very helpful."

After the meeting with Anil, Jenny packed her laptop and headed back to the hotel. She was feeling pretty tired from last night's travel and today's meetings. She was ready for dinner and bed. Tomorrow would be a quick day starting with a meeting with Mark and Tim, sitting in on a few more design sessions, and then the drive back to the airport and the late night flight home.

This isn't a popularity contest

"Good morning Jenny," Tim grinned. "How did you like the hotel?"

"It's fine. I've seen worse," Jenny replied. "At least the hot breakfast is good – and free, too."

"Nothing like the little things to smooth the travel wrinkles," agreed Tim. "Speaking of smooth, I can't say the same for the FirstCorp project team. If this were a popularity contest, I bet you wouldn't even come in as runner-up for suggesting that we come up here for the design session."

"That is what I hear, too," Jenny chuckled. "But you folks are not paying me to be popular."

"Ain't that the truth," Mark chimed in. *"So what do you want to talk about this fine morning?"*

"Well, mainly I just wanted to get your overall impressions of the project at this point in time," answered Jenny.

"Jenny, you were in the status meeting yesterday," Mark said seriously, *"and as you heard, the project is green and on track. What's to worry about?"*

"Green isn't always really green," cautioned Jenny. *"Honestly, don't you guys have any concerns? I observed several issues with acceptance of the tools and technologies in the technical design sessions."*

"I'm not sure what you mean," Tim said quickly. *"You know how those people are: slow to accept change."*

"Yes, I sure do," agreed Jenny. *"But they seemed pretty intent on keeping with their tools despite the fact that BigSI offers some better technologies that will help standardize the business processes and streamline operations."*

"Jenny, I'm really not too concerned about that," Tim said condescendingly. *"Anything else?"*

"Actually there is," Jenny smiled, trying to keep an open dialog with Tim. *"I caught up with Maureen. She is concerned that converting to FirstCorp's systems would be a step backwards technologically. And, after meeting with Anil, we should be aware he is worried about the availability and commitment of both the FirstCorp and the DataTech project team resources."*

"Is that right?" Tim was close to a sneer. *"Like I said before, our project is still on track and reporting green. I think Anil and Maureen need to concentrate on the task at hand. They seemed concerned about bigger picture items that, frankly, are beyond their control."*

"But don't you think the executive committee should be apprised of these issues?" Jenny asked. *"Even though the project is green, it can quickly turn yellow and red."*

"Yeah," Mark interjected. *"We know, we know. Nobody likes surprises."*

"I'm not too worried about it, Jenny," Tim fired his final shot. "Document your concerns in your report if you must, but remember, Bill is not around to take them at face value."

Oh boy, Jenny thought, no sense fighting back today. It would be futile, but these are valid concerns and ones that could cause the reopening of the whole strategy of the project. Jenny couldn't help but wonder why Tim was so defensive. She knew that while things looked good today, potential trouble lay ahead.

Nobody says you can't change directions if it makes sense or potentially could save money, Jenny thought to herself. Why would you want to go backwards, just to re-implement the same functionality later?

"Well, thanks for your time this morning," Jenny said, as she zipped up her portfolio. "I want to make the next design session and then head on out to the airport. My flight's at 5:00 p.m."

"Must be nice to just pop in and out like that," Mark jabbed.

"See you guys later," Jenny replied, meeting his sarcasm with a smile.

"Have a good trip," Tim said, as if all was well.

After the design session was over, Jenny packed up and headed for Anil and Maureen's cubicles to say goodbye. She discovered that Tim had already stopped by to tell them that he had spoken with her and that the chances of changing the implementation order or getting more resources for the project were slim to none. Great, Jenny thought, he isn't going to make this any easier.

"My report is to be independent and it will be objective," Jenny said as she turned to leave Anil and Maureen. "Rest assured that if your concerns are valid, they will be substantiated in the report."

Jenny made the hour-long drive to the airport, returned the rental car and arrived at the gate with ten minutes to spare. After buying a granola bar and an apple, she opened her laptop to summarize the main findings of the trip:

1. DataTech is more advanced than FirstCorp in terms of the use of the technology and its application to business processes. The order of the upgrade should be reconsidered.
2. The key project team resources are stretched thin and oversched-uled. This is resulting in the delay of the deliverable reviews.
3. The project management team is not collaborating on solution development. FirstCorp is driving it.

As Jenny finished typing, the gate agent announced that it was time to board the plane. She shut down her laptop and decided not to turn it back on until tomorrow. She needed a strategy to effectively communicate her findings and gain the consensus to help the project change directions. She knew that until she figured that out, the rest of the report did not matter.

The obligatory pyramid diagram

Jenny arrived for breakfast early, figuring she could organize herself before Bill arrived. But, as she walked through the door, she saw Bill already sitting in a booth drinking coffee and reading the newspaper. He looked relaxed, alert and like he had been up for hours.

"Well, I see you're still an early riser, Bill," Jenny smiled as she slipped into the booth. "I thought that now you are semi-retired, you'd be roll-ing out of bed around 10:00 a.m."

"And miss half the day?" Bill laughed. "That is 'so not me' as my teenaged daughter would say. Plus, I have enough to keep me busy. I'm certainly not retiring to Boca Raton anytime soon."

As the waitress walked by, Jenny signaled for coffee and a menu.

"So how was the trip to the colder climate?" Bill asked. "Sounds like the FirstCorp team is not thrilled with your idea of holding the design sessions in the middle of the country."

"Actually Bill, it was Anil's idea, but it has been pinned to me," Jenny grinned. "And, in reality, I have probably saved FirstCorp a few dollars in project delays."

"I know," Bill took a sip of coffee, staring at her over the cup. "I'm just jerking your chain, Jenny. So what's up?"

"Well, first off, thanks for having breakfast with me," Jenny began. "I know that you are no longer involved, but I really need some guidance. I feel confident in my findings and recommendations, but I am not sure how to effectively communicate them. Tim seems intent on torpedoing me every chance he gets."

"That's not surprising," Bill commented. "I read your findings in the e-mail you sent me. You know, Jenny, you're bringing up some pretty weighty issues. I can see why Tim is concerned – plus his ego still may be a bit bruised."

"You did hire me to be objective, didn't you?" Jenny pointed out.

"That is true," Bill agreed. "But you also know that now I can't help you from the inside. What I can do is give you my best advice."

"Bill, that is all I am wishing for," Jenny said earnestly.

"It's time we put it all together," said Bill, reaching in his breast pocket for a pen and the paper napkin off the table. "No good management theory is worth its salt without the obligatory pyramid diagram ... so here it is. I think it's the best way to depict the process for building consensus and implementing project solutions."

"The intervention process pyramid has three layers: building the foundation, navigating the organization and implementing the solution," Bill said, as he drew a pyramid divided into three horizontal layers. He labeled the layers starting at the bottom: building the foundation, navigating the organization and implementing the solution.

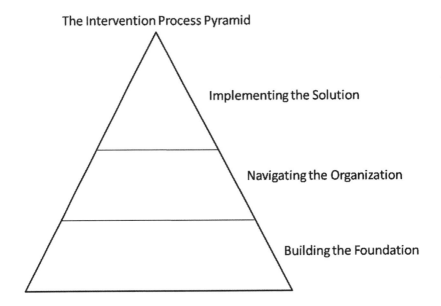

The Intervention Process Pyramid

Implementing the Solution

Navigating the Organization

Building the Foundation

Building the foundation

"**A**s you know, all good relationships are based on trust and credibility," Bill explained. "Trust and credibility are best established through a person's attributes, behaviors and actions. Obviously you were selected for this project because you already have the experience and credentials needed for the job — which provided you with initial credibility. But, as you learned in the first assessment the hard way, if your attitudes and behaviors fail to establish a rapport and relationship of trust with the project team, your credibility is all for naught. To build a foundation for successful intervention, you need to begin with attributes and behaviors that you use to build trust and credibility.*

"I know this is repeating what we discussed in the cafeteria that afternoon, but the main attributes that you need are to be analytical, objective and diplomatic."

"Bill, I'd like to add strategic to that as well," Jenny said, remembering her thoughts on the plane.

"Not sure how I missed that one, but you're right, let's add strategic to the list," Bill said, as he drew a rectangle with four boxes and wrote the words: objective, analytic, diplomatic and strategic.

Objective	Analytic
Diplomatic	Strategic

"Now let's talk about behaviors," Bill said, after the waitress took the breakfast order of spinach omelets and English muffins.

"To be successful, you need to master several personal behaviors in order to achieve the desired goal: listening, seeking to understand, humility and compromise. Within the context of the four behaviors is their interrelationship. There is no hard stop to one behavior before another begins." Bill took another sip of his coffee and signaled the waitress for more. "For example, in seeking to understand an issue, listen well and carefully to what is said – and not said. In approaching a compromise, you need to disarm the natural oppositional response of resisting interference with humility."

"Yes, I agree with you there, Bill," Jenny remarked. "I thought through these behaviors and did my best to use them when I was onsite at DataTech."

"That's great, Jenny. It's probably why you had a good visit and were able to build a rapport with Maureen and Anil," Bill said, as he continued drawing on the napkin.

"This diagram shows you the interrelationships of the four interventionist behaviors that I believe will net you the greatest return: listening, understanding, compromise, and humility," Bill said as he wrote the four words: listening, understanding, humility and compromise.

He connected each word with lines that had arrows at both ends to indicate the continuity of the behaviors.

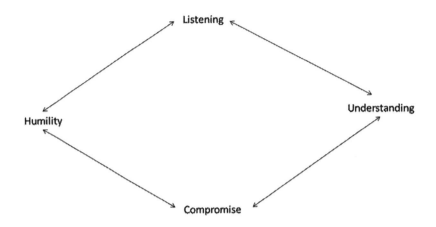

Listening

"The first key behavior of the interventionist is listening. Many people don't actually listen to conversations or to what people are trying to communicate to them. This practice is described as active listening versus passive listening. An active listener is paying attention to the words that are being said, the voice tone and inflection of the speaker and the nonverbal cues as well. Passive listening is hearing the words, but rather than processing the words, you're already working on the solution in your head," Bill explained.

"There are consultants who believe that they have the answers to their client problems before they walk in the door," Bill went on. "While it's not unrealistic that the consultant, based on experience and knowledge may have a pretty good understanding of what the issues are and what the potential solutions may be, he or she would be remiss by not actually listening to the client. Remiss in not only gaining a full understanding of the situation, but also in building the credibility and trust needed to establish the relationship and implement their solutions."

"Just like CYA Partners," Jenny said.

"Exactly," Bill said, cracking a smile as breakfast arrived.

"Miss?" Jenny spoke to the waitress, "could we please have a couple of extra napkins?"

Understanding

"**E**ssential to your role as an interventionist is understanding." Bill took a bite of his English muffin. "It is important to try and seek to understand the point of view of the person you that you are interviewing, the specifics of the project and the dynamics of the overall organization. All of these factors are critical in determining not only the current state of the project, but also essential for developing a strategy to implement change."

"I agree, Bill," said Jenny, sipping her orange juice. "Part of my strategy at FirstTech was not only to identify the role of the person and the project environment, but also to place myself in that person's shoes. By asking questions designed to better understand the other person's concerns, fears and motivations, I gained a better sense of the reality of the situation. In addition, it furthered my credibility and respect with the project team member because of my interest in them and my desire to understand their point of view."

"Jenny, from the first time that you met me, I have maintained that a common denominator in project failures is the human factor," Bill reminded her. "Using these behavior traits lets you really hear and truly understand what your project team members are telling you. It is a major step in intervening before failure becomes a reality."

Humility

"**O**K, I'm with you so far, but what about humility?" asked Jenny, her fork in mid-air. "Can you be an expert and be humble? This is something I am really struggling with. To be honest, I had to bite my tongue in the last meeting with Tim."

"Jenny, the resounding answer is yes," Bill declared. "And that is why the third behavior of a successful interventionist is humility. Being humble in approaching the client's issues – without arrogance, impatience or condescension – is essential to the collaborative intervention process. Because the interventionist is an outsider to the project, the organization and to the members of the team, coming into the situation with guns loaded will only cause people to withdraw from discussions or be resistant to you and any hope of solution. Bringing a sense of humility to the table creates the perception of being genuine – genuine in the sense that you are there to help identify and solve problems on the client's behalf and not your own ego.

"You may still have your work cut out for you with Tim, but being humble will help," Bill finished.

"Definitely. I can see, as with the other behaviors, humility is crucial to establishing rapport and creating trust by letting others know that you have their best interests at heart," Jenny said, understanding what she needed to do next with Tim. She took another bite of her omelet.

Compromise

"**B**ut I'm not sure about compromise, Bill. You know my favorite definition of compromise," Jenny grinned, "is that upon reaching it, no one is truly happy."

"I like that," Bill grinned. "I may have to use that line myself. But think about it: the ability to compromise puts the behaviors of listening, understanding and humility into action. Just as diplomacy and negotiation are important in reaching consensus among disparate groups, reaching consensus is often not possible without the willingness to compromise. Each party has to give up something to reach a solution – which is often the case. It can be any party in the discussion, including the interventionist, who may have to yield parts of his or her position to achieve consensus for workable solutions to project problems."

Bill put down his fork and picked up his pen to add two new lines dividing the first section of the pyramid. He wrote the words: attributes and behaviors in the bottom of the pyramid and trust and credibility in the section above it. "By exhibiting the attributes and behaviors of a successful interventionist, you'll build the foundation of trust and credibility required to navigate the organization and implement solutions," he explained.

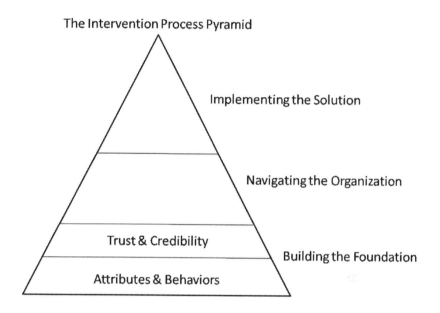

The Intervention Process Pyramid

Implementing the Solution

Navigating the Organization

Trust & Credibility

Building the Foundation

Attributes & Behaviors

Navigating the organization

Jenny nodded her head. "I got it so far," she said. "But I feel like much of what I have accomplished is just a start."

"You know, I believe you're right," Bill began. "Project teams are complicated and consist of a variety of players and participants ranging from executives, project managers, team leads, consulting executives, consultants, independent contractors and vendor partners. All of these people need to be pointed in the same direction for the success of the project. But how is this accomplished, who is charge and how are decisions made?"

"That is exactly what Anil, Maureen and I are all trying to figure out," Jenny said in frustration. "In absence of process, Tim is simply taking over."

"So where do I start?" Jenny asked, feeling lost. "This information is crucial for me to be effective. The tricky part is that this information will ultimately vary from project to project and from organization to organization and a lot of the players are new to me. I'm also sensing a lot of formal power versus informal power in the form of influencers."

"Well," Bill answered, "based on my experience, Jenny, there are three things that you can do to determine how decisions are made:

1. **Start with the obvious.** As simple as it may sound, start with information contained in the project documents such as the needs assessment, project plan or charter. These documents should contain at a minimum: the definition of project team member's roles and responsibilities, the organization chart, issue resolution process and project governance structure.

2. **Validate the information through observations and interviews.** Ask questions such as 'Can you make that decision?' 'Who made that decision?' 'What is that person's role?' Once decision makers start to emerge, ask questions to determine who the influencers are, such as 'Whose advice does the decision maker seek?' or 'What is their process for gathering information?'

3. **Observe how decisions are made.** As part of the assessment, attend a project governance meeting or steering committee meeting. Observe the process and communication patterns of the executives. For some organizations, such as vendors or consulting firms, the process is easy to assess, as there is usually just one person in charge of the account. Inside of an organization, the decision making power will be harder to diagnose.

"Good places to look for answers about how decision making occurs are internal politics, past success and funding," Bill continued. "Typically, executives who have had past project success will have the organizational credibility to either make the decisions or influence them. Also, you can't ignore who is funding the project as well as the dynamics among internal departments. There are situations where managers and directors do not communicate with each other, and as a result, have completely different perceptions of issues and resolution. In cases like this, where stalemates exist, you may have to go higher to executives who are not involved in the project to act as a tie-breaker."

"I guess you are right, Bill," Jenny said wistfully. "It was just easier when it was either you or Cindy making all the decisions."

"You can't rely on that anymore," Bill replied, "but from the steps above you should be able to map out the process required to start communicating issues and building consensus for issue resolution. But be careful, Jenny, you are treading into new territory. Be sure to maintain your foundation attributes and behaviors. You can see how Tim tried to sabotage your relationship with Maureen and Anil when you were leaving DataTech."

"Yes, you are right, Bill," Jenny responded. "But we both know the sources of power can change quickly in the form of a resignation, reassignment or retirement of a key project executive leaving the project with an entirely new landscape. If that is the case, I can use the knowledge of the power structure as protection against project failure due to unforeseen change."

Conducting mini-briefings

Jenny pushed her plate to the side, put her elbows on the table and rested her chin on her hands.

"OK, so after I figure out how decisions are made, Bill, do I just present my findings to the executive committee?" Jenny asked. "I'm not sure that will fly. In fact, you've always said 'When you are reviewing findings with project team members and executives, there shouldn't be any surprises.' No wait, let me restate that: '... there should NEVER be any surprises.' Is that correct?"

"Yes, and you do have a good memory," Bill smiled at Jenny. "Unless the news is overwhelmingly good – like winning the lottery – it is best that everyone is prepared and aware of any issues before meeting with the group as a whole. The best way to accomplish this is through mini-briefings similar to our process for conducting the intervention on the original implementation when we discussed our proposed recommendations and got buy-in from individuals before we met as a group – and long before we talked to Cindy.

"You can schedule a mini-briefing or just have an informal conversation over lunch or coffee. What's important is that you provide an overview of the assessment and any potential recommendations. This pre-discussion serves several purposes:

1. **No surprises.** People have an opportunity to be prepared for a difficult discussion if necessary.

2. **Validate your findings**. It is possible that you may have misinterpreted or have been given incorrect information. If either is the case, then you will save yourself from an embarrassing situation and keep your credibility intact by validating your position ahead of time.

3. **Provide an opportunity to fix a problem**. Oftentimes, executives may be unaware of a particular issue and the fix may be relatively simple. By providing them an opportunity to fix a problem, you are saving them from a potentially uncomfortable situation while building trust with that individual.

4. **Provide an opportunity to start thinking.** Whether it's about potential solutions or digesting your recommendations, getting

everyone on the same page ahead of time helps when you get a group of executives together. If potential solutions are complicated, it is good for people to think through them before a meeting. It helps everyone to understand the solution and determine the pros and cons, preventing rash decisions that may be pressured by an executive in a position of power."

"Yes, I can see how that will work and given the difference of opinions – why it is necessary," Jenny remarked, as Bill penned the words: *identify decision making process* and *conduct mini-briefings* to the pyramid.

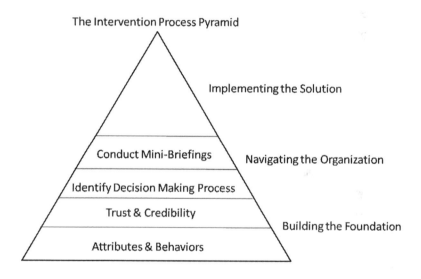

The Intervention Process Pyramid

Implementing the Solution

Conduct Mini-Briefings — Navigating the Organization

Identify Decision Making Process

Trust & Credibility

Attributes & Behaviors — Building the Foundation

Implementing the solution

"**S**o by now I have built the foundation consisting of trust and credibility and navigated the organization by determining the decision making process," Jenny counted each stage on her fingers. "Next, I've validated my findings through the mini-briefings. So what's left?"

"I thought you'd never ask," Bill chuckled. "Now it's time to assemble the project team and sponsors in order to present your findings *and develop the action plan for solution implementation. But how do you do it?*

"Start by communicating the findings. Your project assessment report will most likely contain good and bad news. Since communicating bad or less than positive news to people is never easy, here are some guidelines that have worked for me:

1. **Soften the blow.** *Use pre-meetings to inform everyone involved and avoid surprises.*

2. **Set the stage.** *First discuss your process and how you reached your findings. Let people know what documentation you reviewed and whom you have interviewed.*

3. **Start with good news.** *Positively acknowledge people's accomplishments, achievements and cooperation in the assessment process.*

4. **State the facts.** *Pure and simple, without emotion or finger pointing. To quote a popular phrase 'It is what it is.' Mention (without names) any opposing views or disagreements to your findings that you sensed from the mini-briefings.*

5. **Ask for input.** *Let people state their views if they disagree, but always focus on facts, not emotions.*

6. **Present your recommendations.** *There is nothing worse than someone who points out flaws without solutions. If it is a difficult problem with alternative solutions, outline them. And, if you truly cannot solve the problem, state that and lead a discussion to come up with solutions.*

"After you've communicated your findings, the final part of solution implementation is to negotiate solutions. It is probable that all of your

recommendations will not be accepted or possible, given the parame-
ters of the project. The key is to gain consensus that your findings have
created legitimate concerns and need to be addressed. Any number
of reasons – time, budget or politics – may prevent the implementa-
tion of the solution as you see it. Therefore it's important to work with
the executive team to, at an absolute minimum, acknowledge the risk,
but ideally, to find alternative solutions to project issues. The solutions
should be documented, added to the project plan or action item log
and reviewed at the next point in time assessment," Bill said, as he
completed the pyramid.

The Intervention Process Pyramid

Negotiate Solutions — Implementing the Solution
Communicate Findings
Conduct Mini-Briefings — Navigating the Organization
Identify Decision Making Process
Trust & Credibility — Building the Foundation
Attributes & Behaviors

"That makes sense," Jenny said, as she placed the napkins side-by-
side to form the complete picture of the intervention process.

The Intervention Process Pyramid

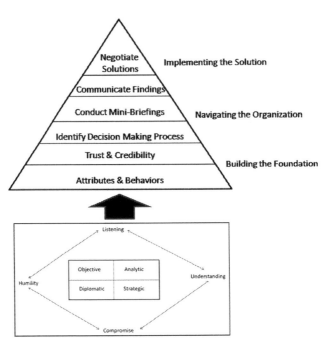

Attributes & Behaviors of the Interventionist

"I like it," Bill said, sipping the last of his coffee and signaling the waitress for more. "Here is the most important thing I can teach you." He set his coffee cup back down on the saucer and looked directly at Jenny.

"In becoming an interventionist, Jenny, you will come to understand the difference between being a project manager and being a leader. Project managers process tasks that organize the implementation environment. Leaders conduct those same tasks while also inspiring and motivating the team they oversee. Project managers cope with complexity, but leaders cope with change. Project managers participate in predetermined tasks of planning, organizing, and controlling the project. In contrast, the leader, as interventionist, approaches the

project implementation through a higher order by setting the direction, aligning the people, and assuring overall project success."

"I never thought of it that way," Jenny said slowly, as a light bulb went on in her head. "If I need to truly intervene on the FirstCorp project, I'm going to have to be the leader."

"That's right," Bill smiled, "but the tricky part is going to be doing it in the context of the interventionist."

The intervention

After talking to Bill, Jenny retreated to her home office to study the FirstCorp situation. Toby, happy to see her back home, wagged his tail and threw his large, fluffy body down on the rug at her feet. She thought back to her trip to DataTech.

"Maureen and Anil agreed with me, in fact, in some ways, I was just championing their recommendations," Jenny said to herself as she scratched Toby's massive head. If dogs could smile, he would be a perfect example.

Jenny was still trying to figure out how the decisions were made at FirstCorp. Some of her recommendations could be made at the project team level, but if there was a need to go back and adjust the overall strategy, then that decision would have to be made by the executive committee members: Brett and Angie from FirstCorp, Mel from DataTech, and Terry from BigSI.

Since Jenny considered Maureen and Anil to be in favor of changing the project direction, she started with them. To navigate the organization, she would need to understand the executive committee structure and relationship dynamics.

Taking advantage of the short workweek due to the Thanksgiving holiday, Jenny realized that this was an opportune time to talk with the project team because no one would be traveling to DataTech this week. There would be no distractions about the potential bad weather or travel issues.

Jenny scrolled through her contact list on her smartphone and found Maureen's name. At the same time, she sent an e-mail to Anil requesting a call later today.

"Hi Maureen, this is Jenny," she said.

"Hey Jenny, how is it going?" Maureen replied. "Are you getting ready for the holiday?"

"Yes, but nothing fancy this year. Just turkey and trimmings with the family – who all happen to live in town," Jenny said with a smile. "Fortunately, we don't have to travel."

"Must be nice," Maureen sighed, "we're heading to Minnesota on Wednesday morning."

"Well, travel safely," Jenny responded. "I hope you have a good time."

"Thanks, Jenny," Maureen said. "What's up?"

"Did you have a chance to read my preliminary report?" Jenny asked.

"Yes, I did," Maureen paused. "I liked your recommendations – but I don't think they will fly."

Jenny was surprised. "Why not?"

"Well, I agree with them," Maureen said, obviously uncomfortable. "But I don't think Tim will present them to the executive committee."

"Have you shared the recommendations with Mel?" Jenny queried. "He is the DataTech representative on the executive committee, right?"

"Yes, he is and no, I haven't shared your report," Maureen answered. "Honestly, I didn't think that would be appropriate. But Mel does know who you are – you're definitely on his radar. He asked me how your visit went."

"Well, I guess that's positive," Jenny said and took a deep breath before continuing. "Look Maureen, I don't want to put you in a difficult position and I understand if you aren't comfortable talking to Mel, but I'd like to talk to him. I'm planning to fly up to your offices again the week after the holiday for the executive committee meeting. Would you make an introduction for me or set up a meeting with Mel and me? You are welcome to attend if you wish."

"Of course, I can make the introduction, Jenny," Maureen answered. "But I'm not sure if I want to attend the meeting – that may not look so good with Tim."

"No problem, I appreciate your help, Maureen," Jenny said. "Enjoy the holidays."

"You, too." Maureen ended the call.

Energized, Jenny grabbed her portfolio, keys and cell phone to head to the coffee shop. She felt like she had a shot of convincing DataTech and BigSI about her recommendations, but she needed to figure out FirstCorp.

This is so ironic, Jenny thought, FirstCorp is the organization that I thought I knew best. It's funny how things change when key people leave or change roles.

One thing was clear to Jenny: Tim was the major obstacle. She figured she could go around or over him if she had to, but that could easily backfire. Jenny considered her odds. She wasn't sure where Brett stood. Angie was a wild card because of her reputation, but Jenny couldn't help but think that because Angie was from DataTech, she would understand the productivity gains they would be sacrificing if they stayed with the current plan.

I need to find a way to get Tim to the table, Jenny thought as she drove to the coffee shop. Mark had agreed to meet her there on his way into the office. Traffic was light because school was out for the holidays. She made the drive in record time. Mark was her best chance and she knew this would be a good time to talk with Mark away from Tim to find out where he stood on the issues.

"Hey Jenny," Mark grinned, already standing in line.

"No Jenny, Jen-Jen-Jen today?" Jenny laughed. "Are you feeling OK?"

"I thought I'd cut you a break," he said seriously. "I know we've been a bit tough on you."

"Not you so much as Tim," Jenny retorted with a smile.

"That is true," Mark agreed, handing her a coffee as they walked to an open table.

"Mark, have you had a chance to read my e-mail with the preliminary findings and recommendations?" Jenny asked.

"I sure did," Mark said emphatically. "I gotta say, you sure are aiming high. Honestly, Jenny, I just don't get the whole issue – the project is on track."

"Mark, even though everything is on track right now, it seems to me that the train is heading in the wrong direction," Jenny explained, setting her coffee cup down and looking directly at Mark. "While I definitely understand that this isn't what everyone wants to hear – especially when they have been told everything is just fine, I've never said anybody isn't working hard or doing a good job.

"I just think you guys need to step back and make sure that the strategy is correct," Jenny finished firmly, and then grinned. "At the end of the day, Mark, if I don't point this out, I'm not doing what I've been hired to do."

Mark cleared his throat. "I understand what you are saying, Jenny, but for the most part, this is Tim's project. He is the one that championed the strategy."

Interesting, Jenny thought as she stirred her coffee. No wonder he doesn't want to change course and is trying to strong-arm everyone. This was his baby. Now it all makes sense. I've got to help make the change, while saving face for Tim.

"Mark, what do you really think?" She took another sip of coffee, eyeing him over the top of the mug.

"I think your idea is at least worth looking into," Mark said, without hesitation.

"I appreciate that, Mark," Jenny said earnestly. "You have to understand that things change, the environment changes, executives change. The strategy you folks came up with six months ago was valid then, I even said so in my first report. But after digging deeper, it makes more

BECOMING AN INTERVENTIONIST

sense at this point to change direction. I firmly believe everyone will be more successful because of it."

"Tell you what, I'll talk to Tim and see where his head is on this," Mark offered, "but I don't think he is going to change his mind."

"I appreciate you at least considering the effort," Jenny smiled.

"Anything for you, Jenny, Jen-Jen-Jen," Mark grinned for the first time that morning. "I need to get to the office before they call a search party."

"There's the old Mark I know," Jenny laughed, relieved at the change in Mark's tone. "And thanks for the coffee."

Two down and one to go

Jenny remained in the nearly empty coffee shop for another latte after Mark left. The shop was warm and inviting, with enough privacy for a discussion, Wi-Fi and wonderful bagels. In fact, it was becoming an interim office for her on the days she didn't go into FirstCorp.

Jenny tapped Anil's number into her smartphone.

"Hello, this is Anil," the familiar deep voice answered.

"Hey Anil, it's Jenny," she said.

"Hey Jenny, how's it going in the sunny South?"

"Pretty good," she replied. " Just trying to get ready for the holiday."

"Me, too," he responded. "So what's up?"

"Anil, thanks for taking a few minutes to chat," Jenny began. "I spoke with Maureen this morning."

"Yes, I know," Anil said. "She gave me a call. Do you really think you can convince the EC to change the project direction to upgrade DataTech first, and then convert FirstCorp to DataTech's system?"

"I'm going to give it a try," Jenny said.

"I really do think it makes sense and I've already spoken with Terry," Anil went on. "He is on board with it. To be honest, it's actually something that he has been talking about for some time."

"Well, that is good to hear," Jenny grinned, pleased with the revelation that she had another ally. "Has Terry presented this idea to the executive committee?"

"No he hasn't been convinced that the time was right and wasn't sure of all of the players," Anil responded thoughtfully. "He thinks Brett is against it based on a conversation they had at the BusinessWare conference. And frankly, he was scared of Bill."

"Really?" Jenny was surprised.

"Yes," Anil explained, "but now that Angie is involved, he's a little more confident. In fact, he told me that he would support your recommendation."

"That's great, Anil," said Jenny, "but what about Mel?"

"Mel's probably on board but not willing to stick his neck out," Anil observed, "given all the rumors about job cuts with the merger, I don't think he is going to make any bold moves."

"I can understand that," Jenny agreed. "Good to know."

"Listen Jenny, I've got a conference call coming through that I need to be on," Anil said, and warned, "just know that even though you have our support, you need to tread lightly. This could well be a very touchy subject with FirstCorp."

"Thanks for the heads-up, Anil," Jenny replied. "I am well aware of that."

As Jenny hung up the phone, she knew that she needed to pull a rabbit of out her hat. What would Bill do? Jenny wondered. Then it came to her and she began typing her final report before heading back to her house.

Jenny takes a deep breath ...

The Thanksgiving holidays flew by and before Jenny knew it, she was on the road driving from Milwaukee to the DataTech site. The executive committee meeting was at 4:00 p.m. that day. Maureen had told her that Mel was unavailable to meet with her before the meeting, but he had seen a copy of the recommenda-tions. Maureen said that she thought he was on board, but confirmed what Anil had said in that she didn't think that he would stick his neck out.

There was a ten o'clock pre-meeting with Tim, Mark, Maureen and Anil to prep for the executive committee meeting. Jenny's flight had arrived late. She worried that she might miss the beginning of the meeting. Great, Jenny said to herself, just what I need.

She called Maureen to let her know she was running late.

Jenny hurried through the front door at 10:10 a.m., but as luck would have it, Maureen had told Tim she needed to deal with an urgent issue and requested that the meeting be delayed until 10:30 a.m. Jenny wasn't sure if there really was an issue or if Maureen just covered for her – either way, Jenny was grateful.

Taking advantage of the extra few moments, Jenny unpacked her laptop, gathered her handouts, refilled her bottle of water and walked into the meeting room promptly at half-past ten and settled into her chair as everyone else arrived.

Tim started the meeting by passing out the EC Status report and the dashboard that showed an overall status of green. Here we go again, Jenny thought. For the next fifteen minutes, they walked through the agenda items as the project team agreed on who would say what and tweaking some of the wording. At the very bottom of the meeting agenda was the last item: the project assurance audit report with Jenny's name next to it.

Finally, it was her turn. Jenny took a deep breath and passed out her report. She began by praising the project team for the work they had accomplished and their ability to keep the project on track so far. Jenny started with her findings about the order of the implementation of the project resources.

"As part of my final report, which this group hasn't seen yet," Jenny began, "I included a study of the additional costs and loss of *functionality that FirstCorp would realize if they continued down their current path. I've also included an analysis of the original proposed project resources versus the actual commitments of the people on the team."*

Jenny continued her summary. "Based on facts and a solid analysis, it is clear to me that a change in direction is necessary and that the project is understaffed," she finished.

The silence in the room was deafening. Maureen and Anil cracked small smiles.

Tim finally spoke. "Jenny, thanks for your recommendations and analysis," he said, looking up from her report. "Given the scope and scale of what you are recommending, this group doesn't have the authority to make the decisions that you are recommending," he paused for a long moment before resuming. "I think that you know that some of us support your findings and some of us do not. It will be up to the executive committee to decide. At the very least, it should be an interesting meeting this afternoon."

"See you at 4:00 p.m."

No wishing required

*J*enny walked in the front door from her morning jog hearing her cell phone ringing from the kitchen counter. She didn't recognize the number, but the area code was in South Carolina.

"Hello, this is Jenny," she said as she opened the cabinet to pull out a bagel.

"Jenny, it's Bill Parker."

"Bill Parker, how are you doing?" Jenny stopped mid-way across the kitchen on her way to the toaster. "I haven't seen you since we had breakfast and drew all over the napkins," she said with a chuckle. "And you know what? I still have them in my desk – I call it reference material."

"I guess you're right about that – I should feel honored you kept my artwork," Bill laughed in response. "Time sure does fly."

"Are you still retired?" Jenny asked facetiously.

"Semi-retired," Bill responded.

"And what are you doing in South Carolina?" she asked.

"Living the dream," Bill said. "I'm playing golf, fishing, and we bought a pretty little place on Lake Keowee."

"So where exactly is the 'semi' part of semi-retired?" Jenny questioned.

"Well, in my spare time I'm sitting on a few boards and teaching a couple of MBA classes at Clemson," he explained.

"It actually sounds like you're having fun, Bill," Jenny responded.

"I can't complain," Bill chuckled. "By the way, how did things turn out with the FirstCorp/DataTech project?"

"Funny you should ask," Jenny answered. "DataTech just completed the BusinessWare upgrade two weeks ago and FirstCorp is going to start converting to the new platform in a couple months when operations stabilize."

"Well, I guess congratulations are in order," Bill sounded genuinely happy for her. "It appears that your intervention was a success."

"Thanks, Bill. I sure would like to think so," smiled Jenny. "What is interesting is that while it was a lot of work in the early stages, after we closed some of the big gaps things began to go a little easier and I actually spent less time on the project. In fact, I was pretty much wrapped up before the system went live."

"That's the way it should be," Bill responded. "I think what is interesting about project assurance is that the issues will vary from project to project. If you think back to the original project implementation, we had a lot of gaps related to tactical project issues: BusinessWare's involvement, the change management scope, and strategic issues relating to whether we continued on the HR implementation."

"Yeah, I can see that," agreed Jenny. "On this last project, our first issues were tactical – related to connectivity and DataTech's involvement. And then the main issue was strategic, what started out as what seemed to be the right strategy changed as we got into the design sessions. But as the project went on, we dealt with both strategic and tactical issues, but none as big as changing the order of the implementation. I like to think I added value, but in reality, the project team did all the hard work."

"So, how did you get the project team to buy into your ideas?" asked Bill. "The last I heard was that Tim was a major roadblock."

"Let's just chalk it up to a solid business analysis, navigating the organization and figuring out how decisions are made," summarized Jenny. "I knew that if I could show the team real numbers and solid facts, we could take the emotion out of it. Plus, I knew that I had two out of four executive committee members on board with my recommendations. The odds were even, but I figured that Angie would not want to take a step backwards in terms of productivity gains. So I gambled that if that I presented my findings with realistic, go-forward recommendations, I could win her support, too.

"Actually, Bill," Jenny chuckled, "the executive committee meeting was a non-event. Once Tim saw Angie was on board, he did a 360 degree turn and acted like the whole change in strategy was his idea."

"That is no surprise to me," remarked Bill.

"Well, it didn't really bother me that Tim was taking the glory," Jenny went on. "Frankly, I was just happy that they made the right choice. These people worked very hard and made a lot of personal sacrifices for the good of the project. I only had to pop in and out. They deserve the kudos – not me."

"Spoken like a true interventionist," Bill laughed. "Jenny, listen, the reason I'm calling is that I serve on the Board of Zachary Industries now and they have a big transformation project underway. I suggested the need for Project Assurance Services and gave them your name. Is that OK?"

"Sure," exclaimed Jenny. "You know I'd be delighted to help."

"You should be getting a call from Karen, the CIO, sometime this week, but I wanted to alert you first."

"Thanks Bill," Jenny said. "I appreciate it."

"You know, it is actually amazing, looking back at all this," Bill observed, "project assurance is quite valuable to an organization, yet is often misunderstood, overlooked and underutilized. At the board level, I recently learned that 80% of strategic plans fail to be executed. This isn't that far off of the 70% implementation failure rate for IT projects. It begs the question: since the execution of strategic plans is comprised of projects, why wouldn't you want to establish a strategic project assurance structure to improve your chances of success?" Bill mused. "It seems to make perfect sense to me."

"You know what? I wish project assurance was as easy as you make it sound," Jenny said wistfully.

"Jenny, once you have the know-how, the proactive methodology and the attributes of an interventionist," Bill said with a smile, "there's no wishing required."

REFERENCES

1. Outsourcing: Industrialize your applications delivery to achieve high performance. Accenture 2008

2. Wikipedia - (Sommerville, Ian (2007) [1982]. "4.1.1. The Waterfall Model". Software engineering (8th ed.). Harlow: Addison Wesley. pp. 66f. ISBN 0-321-31379-8.) http://en.wikipedia.org/wiki/Waterfall_model#Criticism

3. Wikipedia http://en.wikipedia.org/wiki/Project_ Management_ Professional

4. Wikipedia http://en.wikipedia.org/wiki/IV%26V

Made in the USA
Charleston, SC
26 January 2011